ETHNIC

BY DESIGN

FOR JULIAN

Ethnic by Design
Dinah Hall

Photography by James Merrell
Location researcher **Katrin Cargill**

First published in Great Britain in 1992 by
Mitchell Beazley
an imprint of Reed Consumer Books Ltd
Michelin House, 81 Fulham Road,
London SW3 6RB
and Auckland, Melbourne, Singapore and
Toronto

Design Director **Jacqui Small**
Executive Editor **Judith More**
Art Editor **Trinity Fry**
Editor **Catherine Rubinstein**
Junior Editor **Catherine Smith**
Production **Sarah Schuman**

A CIP record for this book is available from the British
Library

ISBN 1 85732 929 5

Typeset in Gill sans Roman 10/16 and Bembo italic 10/16
by Dorchester Typesetting Group Ltd, Dorchester, Dorset
Origination by Mandarin Offset, Singapore
Printed in Hong Kong

ETHNIC
BY DESIGN

Dinah Hall

Photography by James Merrell

MITCHELL BEAZLEY

CONTENTS

"**I**f we would return to a more healthy condition, we must even be as little children or as savages; we must get rid of the acquired and artificial, and return to and develop normal instincts." Designer Owen Jones, writing in *The Grammar of Ornament* in 1856, anticipated by some 50 years the revolution in perception that was to change the face of Western art and expressed the fundamental conundrum that continues to tease civilization: the more refined and advanced the world becomes, the deeper people need to dig beneath the surface to find their true values. A century after the painter Paul Gaugin dreamt of finding "ancient, sublime, religious things" in Tahiti we are once again searching for the power of the primitive, digging deep into our roots in an inevitable reaction to the surface glossiness of design over the past decades. If Gaugin felt the need to escape from the progress and technology of "civilization" more than 100 years ago, how much more desperate must be our need today, when the computer and the machine threaten to take over completely. As technology becomes capable of creating soulless perfection, so we hunger for imperfection — for the rough beauty that bears the imprint of the fallible human hand.

Previous page and left: In Christian Astuguevieille's Paris apartment the neutral harmony of cased insects, rope creations and African sculptures is offset by the intense blue of the lights.
Right: Grand Parisian architecture is a surprising but stunningly effective backdrop and counterpoint to Astuguevieille's unique coiled designs, inspired by primitive cultures.

During the so-called "yuppie" years of the 1980s, success was the god which had to be placated with designer labels. It was worshipped in two basic forms. There was the rich, flabby look, with its opulent draperies, fat sofas and paint-effect walls, accessorized with antique silver boxes and trinkets from the past; and the rich, lean look, featuring hard metal chairs, Venetian blinds or shades and angular sofas accessorized with all the latest in matte-black technology from Japan's slickest, most contemporary designers.

But despite the designer labels claiming responsibility for what were, in effect, mass-produced items, the human touch — the sense of individual creativity — was somehow lacking from both. The increasing accessibility of far-flung countries and the importation from them of handmade ethnic goods, especially coming at a time of growing ecological awareness, have reinforced the feeling of alienation provoked by that typical designer environment. The veneration in which we held "designer objects" meant that creativity had become a vicarious pleasure: we were capable of appreciating someone else's work, but not of doing "our own thing".

Actually making something with your own hands is an art — maybe more than an art, maybe a basic human need — that the majority of people have all but lost, but which we see still in the ethnic crafts that are passed down through the generations. For instance, those of us who were taught to sew and embroider by our mothers and grandmothers have buried the skill and, partly because of the demands of work, partly through a misplaced ideal of feminism, are not passing it on to our daughters. Of course we can't be expected to

mourn the lost art of darning socks, but when you see the traditional appliqué work of India or Africa and imagine it used in a Western context — to make unique curtains or drapes, perhaps, instead of buying mass-produced mediocrity by the yard or metre — you realize how little of our tremendous creative potential we do in fact use.

The difference between today's revival of interest in ethnic and the much-reviled "hippy ethnic" of the 1960s and early 1970s, with its joss sticks and Indian bedspreads, is that the latter was very much an expression of an alternative culture, a turning-away from society and a form of escapism. But the new ethnic style is not a

Left: In Astuguevieille's hands, craft becomes art. The baskets which line the mantelpiece are intended to look as if they are still in production, a forest of reed warps projecting upward, giving the display the height it needs to fit in with the proportions of the room. They are streaked across with the deep, bright blue that is picked up in the lights, and with which Astuguevieille periodically punctuates the careful neutrals of the apartment, blue being for him "the colour of spring". Even the largest pieces of furniture are covered in rope, proving that the most basic of materials can create the most exotic style.

Below: The walls of Astuguevieille's kitchen, their muted image in keeping with the room's double function as storeroom, are in dramatic contrast to the elegant perfection of the ornate walls in the other rooms of the house.

Above: The raw, natural tones of the apartment even extend to the books — no shiny jackets or bright red spines are allowed to intrude on the neutral colour scheme: perhaps not the best criteria on which to base your literary taste, but effective enough if the volumes are to be used primarily as stands for a collection of artefacts.

Below: The pedestal table and bed play on classical shapes, with an amusing — but perhaps unintentional — allusion to place mats in the weave. The sense of exotic far-flung travel which the bed evokes is picked up in the trunk used as furniture, on which are placed some smaller articles of Astuguevieille's distinctive craft.

Above: Each piece of furniture is as precisely detailed as that of a master carver.

Left: Astuguevieille has tamed the pliant nature of his materials into a strict, tailored asceticism which complements the linear feel of the room. Even the most mundane object takes on an aesthetic cast when mounted in a glass case — an unravelled rush place mat may look squalid on a kitchen table, but it takes on a new significance when seen through the highly individualistic eyes of Astuguevieille.

Below: The classic lines of the armchairs and the squared effect of the white wooden panelling are offset by a glimpse through to cupboard doors painted with softer abstract squiggles.

rejection of the way we live, it is almost a way of coming to terms with it by keeping in touch with our fundamental sensual appetites for beauty and creativity at the same time as making the most of selected aspects of modern life. It is not regressive — in fact it works best in the most modern interiors, where crudeness and sophistication can act as a foil to each other.

Just as interiors in the past reflected the era of colonialism — the British in India, the French in North Africa, the Dutch in Indonesia — so today's interiors inevitably reflect the small world of global travel. As long-haul journeys become more commonplace, homes become more exotic: just as the 18th-century Grand Tour left its legacy of bronze Parthenons, so today's long-distance tourist advertises a global credibility with Thai temple dogs.

But when does ethnic art become the much-disdained "souvenir"? Pieces don't have to be rare or intrepidly acquired to be well worth having — the painter Henri Matisse brought back what were probably quite commonplace vases from Algeria and decorated tiles from Spain, and nobody sneered at him for being a souvenir hunter. Back home, a cheap blue and white Moroccan plate, even though it was one of

hundreds on a market stall, will continue to give the same thrill that made your heart beat faster when you first saw it on the streets of Marrakech. The expensive panic-buy at the airport, however, will always be a souvenir in the worst sense.

Ironically, perhaps, travel can often awaken a dormant appreciation of the traveller's own native culture. It was only after journeying abroad, for instance, that the artist Diego Rivera was jolted into recognizing the primitive splendour of Mexican folklore which thereafter impassioned his paintings. Even Gaugin recognized a primal paradise closer to his doorstep than Tahiti,

Above left and above: The excessive designer-materialism of the 1980s has been followed by a backlash of asceticism, which has left Westerners craving the simple lifestyle — in terms of decoration if not substance — that is endured in the Third World. In her California home, Melanie Martin takes no half-measures, keeping possessions to a minimum for a cool, uncluttered look. The raw, buff-coloured plaster walls subconsciously imitate mud-hut aesthetics, while furniture and furnishings are fashioned entirely out of primitive materials: weathered timber, hewn stone and floursack canvas. Artistic decoration, too, is thoroughly natural, using the full potential of driftwood sculpture and draped African textiles.

Cosy home comforts have been exchanged for a raw style that is as close to living with the elements as you can get without forgoing a house altogether.
Within this gigantic scale, flowers and houseplants would look insignificant; nothing less than trees will do for Melanie Martin.

Left and right: Ironically, for a style that has evolved through poverty, the ethnic look has an understated elegance and even affluence that has successfully shed its hippy connotations. In Melanie Martin's Marin County tract house, recycled timber and driftwood is more effective, and more ecological, than the most exotic of hardwoods. Tailored Western pieces, such as the sofa, need to be kept to a minimum but can work well with a primitive hunk of furniture like the recycled timber table. This is not a style to suit delicate displays of precious knick-knacks. Accessories need to be monumental in size and made from solid natural materials — giant terracotta pots and wicker baskets; smaller pieces should be grouped together. Below: Simple canvas curtains are hung on wooden rods — spears, preferably whittled out of driftwood, could be used as an alternative. The pleasure in the recycled driftwood table, pegged and bolted without the use of glues, is partly psychological, but is also in tune with environmental awareness.

as he found himself first drawn to the tiny Breton fishing village of Pont-Aven, "a place with archaic customs and an atmosphere very different from that of our over-civilized surroundings".

But travel is not a prerequisite of ethnic style. For some designers, the quest for the primitive takes place within themselves, just as it did at the beginning of the 20th century for artists such as Georges Braque and Pablo Picasso. During the 1980s, the French designers Mattia Bonnetti and Elisabeth Garouste were going against the grain of current slickness and producing furniture of startling primitivism, which earned them the nickname *les barbares* (the barbarians). Although not an official movement, neo-primitive design started cropping up all over the world, rooted in the same primal passions. British sculptor Henry Moore described the essential appeal of primitive art in 1941, saying that it "makes a straightforward statement, its primary concern is with the elemental, and its simplicity comes from direct and strong feelings, which is a very different thing from that fashionable simplicity for-its-own-sake which is emptiness."

It is interesting to realise that ethnic cultures, even those from opposite corners of the world, have always shown a striking similarity of expression and inspiration; the ethnic motifs and artefacts from one continent often sit happily with those of

Left: The most poetic houses are those that respond to the environment in which they are built — like designer Ivy Rosequist's Californian cliffside home, where the interior views are as stunning as the oceanscape outside. Convinced that "the interior had to surrender to the environment," Rosequist avoided using colour that might stop the eye inside the house. Nothing tries to compete with nature here, only to learn and borrow from it. Huge chunks of raw timber along with baskets full of brushwood and newspaper blur the distinction between decoration and function. Are they to sit upon, to burn, or to look at? Nature also supplies the best ornaments: the mantelpiece is draped in strips of eucalyptus bark. In the corner a Roman stone basin sits upon a fir beam, while contrasting texture is supplied by the fleece-draped Mexican chair.

Top right: The "moon window" in the hall is large enough to avoid clichéd porthole connotations. The smaller round window is mirrored by the driftwood "sculpture" — actually the bottom of an old wine-press. Beach-scavenging yields the decorative pile of sea-smoothed glass which together with the boulders forms a tablescape straight from nature.

Middle right: Throughout the house the floors are a smooth run of bleached floorboards striped with concrete to expand the illusion of space. Suspended from the ceiling is a Haitian fishnet.

Bottom right: In line with the rest of the house, the sleeping area is simple but monumental: a casual arrangement on the floor with massive fir columns acting as a bedhead.

another. As archaeologist Frank Willett noted in his book *African Art*, "through the working of instinctive sculptural sensibility, the same shapes and form relationships are used to express similar ideas at widely different places and periods in history, so that the same form vision may be seen in a Negro and Viking carving, a Cycladic stone figure and a Nukuoro wooden statuette."

In the United States, Richard Snyder produces sculptural pieces of furniture that British neo-primitive dealer David Gill describes as "an exotic journey in the mind's eye", explaining his belief that "the forms of primitive culture transform and enrich the lifestyle and taste of the most urbane". In Britain, Malcolm Temple — working in the same idiom, and the same area somewhere between sculpture and furniture — describes himself as a "lyrical paganist". Temple believes that in Britain "we have buried our natural culture along with our true senses. The industrial revolution destroyed indigenous cultures — as people moved from the countryside to towns for work, they were displaced from their culture and so the natural paganism of this country was destroyed." Temple feels that in rediscovering his pagan streak he has had to learn to use parts of himself that were previously dormant, that before this happened his work was "very tight, with the emotions withheld" but that the effect of freeing those emotions is "like the desert after rain".

Parisian designer Christian Astuguevieille also makes extraordinary furniture, using an ethnic approach to create his own unique avant-garde style. Although these amazingly detailed string-wrapped chairs, tables and accessories take their original inspiration from the Japanese art of wrapping — which demands a deceptively casual precision as objects are positioned diagonally on the sheet of paper or cloth,

Below left: Surrounding the mantelpiece in British sculptor Malcolm Temple's living room are examples of his work, which share the primitive imagery of early 20th-century artists like the Romanian sculptor Constantin Brancusi. Below right: The focal carved yellow cabinet is christened the "Optimist's House".

Right: Temple, whose jewel-bright hallway is shown here, loves the vivid colours of Saxon and Celtic art. But he believes that his work has benefitted from a variety of ethnic influences, which cannot be differentiated. "All natural art forms have a certain similarity, that particular sort of naive power."

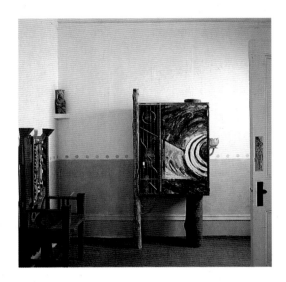

which is then folded over them — the designs have a raw vitality to them, more in keeping with African tribal art. Used in the spare but classical rooms of his grand Parisian apartment, they cross the culture barrier with vivid impact.

The ethnic revival has also meant for many people the return of decoration in a pure form, as opposed to the indigestible decoration of patterned fabrics and carpets. In many ways we are almost returning to a distrust of the machine reminiscent of the 19th-century art critic and social reformer John Ruskin, who believed that "men were not intended to work with the accuracy of tools". And perhaps in our new-found appreciation of wobbly clay pots and bright woven bowls there is also something of Ruskin's naivety in his suggestion that "the right question to ask, respecting all ornament, is simply this: Was it done with enjoyment? Was the carver happy while he was about it?" Often to Western eyes, the crude pottery bowl or the honest basket comes with the intrinsic premise of some blissfully innocent, happy native craftsman toiling away in perfect contentment with his lot in life.

Adolf Loos, an Austrian architect to whom is attributed the phrase "ornament is crime", believed that decoration was a symptom of an uncivilized society. In 1898 he wrote: "The less civilized a people is, the more prodigal it will be with ornament and decoration. The Red Indian covers every object, every boat, every oar, every arrow over and over with ornament. To regard decoration as an advantage is tantamount to remaining on the level of a Red Indian. But the Red Indian within us must be overcome." Nearly a century later we have come full circle — desperately seeking that Red Indian within us.

Above: The bed is constructed from limed pitch pine with a beaten and lacquered lead headboard.

Above left: The "Cage Cabinet" is an assemblage of different elements: the door was cut down from a screen that Temple had made, while the main leg is of plane wood and the thin one is a chestnut pole found on a waste tip.

Right: Totemic sculptures or "love poles" carved from Canadian pitch pine were loosely inspired by Cycladic art. The stereo cabinet is made from packing-case wood and piranha pine, bleached to look as if it had been left out in the sun and then carved in primitive shapes, while the beaten lead panel uses powerful symbols — the eye and the fish — common to almost every culture.

No continent, it could be claimed, has a greater diversity of ethnic styles than America, both North and South. Since the days of Christopher Columbus, its history and its lands have been criss-crossed with the cultural imprints of all the different nationalities who have settled there. In the words of that well-worn cliché, America is the great melting pot of races — and inevitably some of the raw ingredients of those cultures that went into the pot have become diluted in the process.

Yet the grafting of one culture onto another often seems to produce a remarkably hardy plant on which grow particularly

Above: Pre-Columbian statuettes speak with all the powerful primitive force of the ancient civilizations of South America.

exotic blooms. In the southwest of the United States, for instance, the earth-based nobility of Native American style plays host to the baroque and sometimes glitzy grandeur of Spanish colonial, and the resulting blend creates a unique stylistic balance of its own.

For all that variety, however, it is of course Native American culture, despite the battering that it took in the late 19th and early 20th centuries, that forms the bedrock of American ethnic design. Even cowboy style, which is perhaps rooted rather more deeply in the North American subconscious than in historical reality, leans heavily on Native American colours and artefacts, showing cowboy and Indian living more harmoniously together than ever they were allowed to in the old gun-slingin' Westerns.

In Mexico the Spanish influence is more dominant. Nonetheless, here too it is the Central American Indian grounding —

those glimpses of an ancient Aztec civilization — that gives Mexican interiors their particular flavour, that gaudy splendour derived from the curious alliance between pagan and Roman Catholic values.

All ethnic styles take their initial cues from the terrain and what it has to offer in terms of building materials. In the arid southwest, houses were literally moulded from the earth — the use of sun-baked adobe dictated the sensuous curves of walls. Adobe has an enduring romance to it, a natural quality that modern building materials, for all their practical advantages, can never match.

The prairie land where the homesteaders of the late 19th century settled was equally treeless. Their equivalent of adobe was dried sod, which was somewhat optimistically known as "prairie marble". Ecologists out of necessity, they even used buffalo dung for fuel. Modern interpretations of

Previous page: Craftsman-designer Thomas Molesworth defined — even invented — cowboy style. Laura Hunt's house, designed by Molesworth for a client in 1935, still stands as a continuing monument to the man who elevated kitsch fantasy to an art form that expressed the dreams of a nation.

Above: Twiggy Adirondack furniture epitomized the back-to-nature yearnings of urban escapees in search of a rural idyll.

Below: Thomas Molesworth's macho style of furniture with its heavy burls was softened by leather fringing and clever Native American detailing on curtains.

homesteader or cowboy style tend to use timber for fuel as well as building, there being a distinct shortage of buffalo dung around the place these days. Timber at least has a natural quality — if not quite the same rudimentary ring to it as a large lump of dried sod.

But apart from the physical attributes of the land, its less tangible qualities also permeate American ethnic styles in the same way that they have moulded the American character. The interiors have a ruggedness to them, a special affinity with the landscape around them. There will always be comfort, of course, but in an interior that touches the core of American culture, it

Above: Mexican Day of the Dead figures, made to celebrate the day when ancestors are remembered, reflect the thread of fatalism clothed in gaiety that runs through Mexican culture. In contrast to the delicacy of such figures, the furniture is pleasingly rough-hewn and solid.

Left: Spanish colonialism left a heavy legacy of Catholicism and grandly ornate furniture which grew into symbiosis with the more primitive and naive decorative values characteristic of the region's indigenous Mexican Indian culture.

Below: Native America meets Mexico in the gloriously faded colours of Santa Fe style, at one with its desert environment.

Below: For collectors of folk art, such as Chuck Rosenak, the Americas offer rich pickings, ranging from cheap and cheerful naive figures from the South to more rarefied examples of pre-Columbian and Native American art.

parades in tough, macho style — a fringed leather Molesworth armchair that looks as if it could pack a good punch, or a rough, unadorned Mexican wooden settle, rather than any self-indulgent, squashy sofa designed for the pampered form of the typical modern urbanite.

Perhaps it is because these ethnic styles are so deeply rooted in the land that they are the most enduring. Immigrant styles —

Swedish, Russian, Hungarian, Italian, Irish, English, Polish, German — have not had the same impact, despite the pockets of Little Italy or Little Germany. This is perhaps partly because the immigrants themselves were anxious to adopt the lifestyle of their chosen country, but also because imported styles find it harder to take root in alien soil, so far removed from their natural source materials.

Undoubtedly, however, these other ethnic looks will start to flourish once more over the next few years as subsequent generations rediscover and reinterpret their cultural roots. These themes, covered in the European chapter of this book (see pages 70-109), are even now evident in the crafts of immigrant communities in America, although often freshly interpreted and taking on board an element of proper American ruggedness.

The cowboy is the lost dream of America, a potent symbol of the pioneering, free spirit that lies curled up somewhere in the bottom of the American soul, buried beneath the metropolitan layers of sophistication and materialism. Of course, the reality of the cowboy life has been much over-romanticized in Westerns, and the design style that has evolved out of this is not so much a fabrication as a synthesis of artefacts and attitude. Genuine cowboy and Indian relics are put together in a way that expresses a turning away from modern pressures and a yearning for the simple, healthy values of a life as close to the outdoors as you can get indoors. In a sense, this is the American equivalent of the English Country Cottage nostalgia, when "townies" don the superficial skin of a pastoral idyll. But whereas the English effect is one of genteel sentimentality, the American cowboy look has a rugged yet tactile quality — that style mastered by designer Ralph Lauren. Lauren, however, was not the first to reinvent cowboy style. In the 1930s Thomas Canada Molesworth of Cody, Wyoming was creating his extraordinary ranch-style Arts and Crafts furniture, raising kitsch to the realms of art.

Left: The gunslinger silhouette and a surprising use of coloured leather are typical elements of Thomas Molesworth's unique style.

Right: Cowboy kitsch rides roughshod over concepts of restrained "good taste". This corner of a bedroom in Laura Hunt's Colorado ranch is classic Molesworth. Lampshades, chairs, chests of drawers and litter baskets — all were decorated with cowboy imagery which has successfully made the transition from the style wilderness of boys' bedrooms to adult cult status.

In fact, authentic cowboy living at the toughest level was probably closer to the kind of rudimentary interior belonging to a "mountain man" which writer Francis Parkman described evocatively in his book *The Oregon Trail* in 1849: "The walls and floors were of black mud, and the roof of rough timber; there was a huge fireplace made of four flat rocks, picked up on the prairie. An Indian bow and otter-skin quiver, several gaudy articles of Rocky Mountain finery, an Indian medicine-bag, and a pipe and tobacco-pouch garnished the walls, and rifles rested in a corner. There was no furniture except a sort of

Left: Red and white stripes and gingham soften the inevitably macho effect of Molesworth's cowboy-crazed furniture. Bedheads and ends were frequently routed and stained to achieve a frieze effect, while the rawhide lamp here has a burl base.

Right: In the basement games area Molesworth had terrazzo floors patterned with bucking broncos laid by Italian artisans. The straight back and angle-cut arm rests, together with the desperado in the 10-gallon hat, suggest this is a chair for those who take their liquor neat and their poker seriously.

Below: No arty books and exotic flowers for a hunky coffee table like this. The cushions of the leather sofa are faced with 1930s Chimayo weavings from the Ortega workshop in Chimayo, New Mexico.

rough settle, covered with buffalo-robes." Indeed, until Thomas Molesworth fulfilled the fantasy of cowboy style, as Wally Reber and Paul Fees of the Buffalo Bill Historical Center have pointed out, modest Western interiors were far more influenced by the desire of pioneers to recreate the comforts they had left behind them, so that a typical Wyoming ranch at the beginning of the 20th century would probably have been furnished with mission oak furniture, punctuated with the odd antler or twig chair as a kind of vernacular joke. It wasn't until Molesworth was given full rein to unleash his fantasies in the homes of the rich city dwellers who commissioned him to design the furnishings of their rustic retreats that the idea of a "cowboy-style interior" ever really entered design vocabulary.

Molesworth gave reality to the myth and romance of the West, with his macho leather chairs, often incorporating the burl of the wood as a design feature and embellished with images of cowboys or Indian motifs, studs and leather fringing; rawhide lights; chandeliers featuring wrought-iron buffaloes; and horse-head beds. Frequently, his designs overstepped

Above: Collectors of Western Americana, Teresa and Tyler Beard indulge in a textural revival of cowboy style. A collection of studded hide deed boxes sits beside a rawhide lampshade, with leather saddles and chaps used as decorative accessories.

Right: Hunky leather sofas with a framework of undisguised tree trunks were designed by the Beards and made in New Mexico. Junior cowboy boots, deprived of their functional context, are viewed as objects of art and, together with the hats, make an original mantelpiece display.

Below: An unusual still life is comprised of Wyoming antler candlesticks and cowboy boots set against the backdrop of a rare Navajo blanket.

the border between idiom and kitsch, and certainly it would be nice to think he was laughing, as opposed to deadly serious, when he made such items as his elk-foot ashtray. But then only a man with a sense of humour could have made a wing chair where the "wings" were applied moose antlers. The bandy-legged gunslinger silhouette was a favourite Molesworth motif, appearing on everything from chairs to chests of drawers — imagery which fashion dudes today seem to have no problem disassociating from boys'-bedroom style. Less predictable was his colour sense, which stretched from conventional maroons to amazing electric blue and white fringed leather chairs. Where his Wild West enthusiasm was more tamed, it resulted in some quietly stylish effects: simple rawhide curtains, for example, with Native American motifs.

The fullness of Molesworth's style can be seen at its best in Laura Hunt's Colorado ranch, which was designed by him down to the last litter basket and is preserved in perfect detail — a shrine to the myth of the cowboy made real. The effect of his interiors, say Reber and Fees, "is far more

Above: The bedroom cupboard is a modern Texan copy of an old bark-on polework design. Both rocking chair and settee are made by the revived Old Hickory company in Indiana.

Above left: A Mexican pinon-wood cabinet displays a selection of cowboy boots from 1920-60.

Right: The Beards bought the rocking chair off the front porch of a Texan farmhouse — it was made about 60 years ago by some children for their father. The Trigger bedspread is from the 1940s; its cowboy theme is echoed in the stencilled chair-back and the collection of boots and stetsons.

Left: Piled with pillows made from Navajo weavings and draped with warm, clear-coloured Beacon blankets, which were machine-woven from the 1930s through to the 1950s in Indian designs, the Beards' cedar-post bed was made by contemporary Texas craftsmen; similar designs can be made to order through one of two shops specializing in Texan designs. The wardrobe is also native Texan, made in the Hill Country in about 1920, while the cowhide box on top is typical of the travelling trunks used from 1830 to 1910. Next to the wardrobe is a cowhide chair — cowhide, explains Tyler Beard for the benefit of urban dudes, is skin with the hair left on, whereas rawhide has the hair scraped off.

Top right: The Beards' Western obsession extends to the kitschest of crockery. This set was made for an old steakhouse by the Wallace company, who produced hotel and restaurant china between 1938 and 1965. Resting against the rough wooden dresser is a kiva ladder — mainstay of every Santa Fe interior. The kiva was a Pueblo sacred underground chamber, accessible only by ladder and only to men: its sacredness, as the legendary British archaeologist Jacquetta Hawkes put it, "seems to lie half-way between that of a church and that of the most exclusive club in St James's".

Bottom right: The old Texan coffee tins stacked on a lovingly scuffed jam cupboard are prized pieces — because of course few would have survived the garbage dump. The Beards are as enthusiastic about these as they are about the rarest Navajo weaving. The rather romantic cowboy/girl print on the wall behind dates from 1910.

complex than a simple mediation between urban and rural or between the drawing room and the lodge. Like the paintings of the best Western artists, the furniture and roomscapes allow their audience to appreciate without embarrassment the West of romance."

When Molesworth wasn't indulging in whimsical humour, he also made some simple sturdy pieces in lodgepole pine or fir that belonged to the rustic tradition found across America, most notably in the Adirondacks twig and log furniture and in Old Hickory style. For city dwellers who were wealthy enough to retreat to their log cabins at weekends, the furniture they chose had to underline their rejection of — or at least their holiday from — urban comfort and sophistication.

In his book on the rustic tradition in American furniture, Adirondacks expert Craig Gilborn writes: "Twig furniture in the city is a wish; in the Adirondacks years ago it confirmed the completion of the passage from polite society in the city to an informal, somewhat solitary life in the country. Simplicity and primitiveness, to the point of discomfort, were accepted as

integral to a vacation in the woods." Gilborn even makes the playful suggestion that in our response to this furniture there is "under our technological skins" the relic of an ancient belief that trees are inhabited by spirits; we "may be druids at heart". Certainly there is romance in those twigs. Hickory furniture was especially popular in the late 19th century for its "sincere" character, a feeling fuelled by the enthusiasm for Arts and Crafts furniture at the time. It came primarily from Indiana, where the hickory tree is most plentiful. The best-known of its manufacturers was Edmund Brown, whose Old Hickory Chair Company, having closed in the 1950s, has recently been revived. To make the furniture, hickory poles were boiled and bent into shape on metal frames, then fashioned into armchairs, rocking chairs, settees and so on. Some pieces retained the rough outer bark while others had it stripped off; the inner bark thus exposed was used for chair seats, thin strips of it being soaked and then woven together — usually by women and children. Sadly, but inevitably, from the late 1940s this method was replaced with nylon webbing.

Left: The combination of river-rock fireplace, Navajo rugs and the Molesworth cowboy motif on cushions creates a tough yet cosy atmosphere that has its roots deep in Western style.

Right: In the dramatic space of the Gubers' Colorado mountain retreat, moose antler chandeliers, saguaro cacti and Native American artefacts and textiles ground the opulence in accessible ethnic style. Massive pine tree trunks from Colorado, which look as if they have been freshly uprooted from the forest, support the timber structure and emphasize the house's harmony with its surroundings.

Molesworth was not the first to incorporate burls in his designs. The burl, which is like an unsightly but benign tumour on a tree, was to the skilled rustic worker, in Gilborn's words, "what the oyster's pearl is to the jeweller". Cut across, sanded and varnished, they made handsome table tops or pedestal stools.

Today, such rusticity is the height of urban sophistication: if only the few can afford their weekend ranches then the country will have to come to town. Those hard edges of city living are smoothed over with Navajo blankets — the essential Native American complement to Western Americana. As well as blankets, Navajo-inspired pillows are also used by Teresa and Tyler Beard, foremost collectors of cowboy style, whose house in Comanche shows to what extremes their passion runs. At one end of the scale they have native Texan furniture and fittings from the beginning of this century, but they also hoard anything with cowboy imagery, be it a can of baked beans or a 1960s cowboy-pattern blanket from J. C. Penny.

Inevitably cowboy furniture looks best in its native environment, but failing this, the most important mandate has to be texturally sympathetic surroundings — if not wooden walls, then stone or brick. And the same goes for the floors: no self-respecting cowboy should be sinking his heels into carpet pile. Just one note of authenticity it would be as well to avoid, and that's the cocktail bar disguised as The Last Chance Saloon. . . .

Above: A moose stares in astonishment at the extraordinary sight of an antler bursting through a very organic-looking carved door. You know you are truly in cowboy land when the coats hang on horns…. A brightly coloured Native American rug breaks up the dominance of wood.

Above left: Solid unpretentious furniture is upholstered in leather and ponyskin; the matting on the wall is worked in traditional Navajo colours.

The saguaro cactus and stetson are familiar motifs in a cowboy-style interior; but whenever things threaten to become too tough, there is always a Native American blanket to soften the lines. The sepia photographs on the wall are part of a remarkable catalogue of the dying tribes from the late 1800s.

Cowboy style can be hard to track down outside the
United States, and genuine artefacts are increasingly
scarce even within the West. But then much of it is
about attitude: the pioneer spirit that eschews urban
definitions of comfort. Pendleton blankets add the
necessary rough, homespun quality — that feeling of
the outdoors brought inside — which is at the heart
of cowboy-look interiors.

The British archaeologist Jacquetta Hawkes, visiting New Mexico in the 1950s, was one of many to be won over by the region's special charm and character. Her description of the interior of a Spanish/Pueblo-influenced hacienda perfectly sums up the timeless appeal of the intertwined Native American and Spanish cultures. "True it was unkempt, with dust making delicate curtains of cobwebs visible in some of the less used corners, but wonderfully rich, warm and careless. The long living room was furnished with old Spanish and Indian things, painted pottery, rugs, carved images or *santos*, looking glasses and embroidery, and there were also modern American and European paintings and sculpture. Yet as we sat in front of a fire of four-foot logs drinking Old Fashioneds no room could have seemed more harmonious, unaffected and habitable." Earlier in 1930, when the Santa Fe region was already beginning to attract a colony of artists and writers, one of its newcomers, Amelia Hollenbeck, described her ideal house: "something extremely informal that will let us amuse ourselves with old ways and old things, but may heaven preserve it from looking arty! I hope it will look merely natural and sort of inevitable."

Left: Native American arts provide a rich source of artefacts for the collector. All the tribes had different strengths — the Navajo were renowned for their superb red and black lustre pots.
Right: The Navajo were also skilled weavers: in the foreground is an early 1900s chief's blanket; through the doorway is a 1920s Ganado-style example.

Today, Amelia Hollenbeck's "natural and sort of inevitable" has particular resonance. As more is learnt about the Native American way of life, it has become clear that the North American Indians were true ecologists, guardians of the earth that more "modern" cultures have been plundering. To them, animals were "people in the form of animals", and even inanimate things — trees, stones, soil, sun, stars and moon — were viewed as equal inheritors of the universe, to be respected as such.

Art — whether the pottery and jewellery of the southwest, the beadwork of the Plains, Navajo weaving or the basketry of the Cherokees and Hopi — was seen as part of nature, something which was to be integrated into the functional side of life without any of the self-consciousness of Western aesthetics. And yet Native American art has as much power to move as any Renaissance painting.

Jacquetta Hawkes again touches the heart of the matter, describing her feelings on seeing some 1,500-year-old sashes woven by the Basket Maker Indians from the hair of their dogs: "Where did the patterns come from, charged with emotional force to make a woman living as humbly as a badger give hours to their expression? . . . How do they arise in imaginations that are the product of endless generations of animal life among mountains and forests?"

She goes on to compare such handicrafts with the mass of standardized consumer goods in city stores. "Here, a few things supremely satisfying to those who made and enjoyed them, because they expressed something in the being of the makers, of their tribe and its tradition. There, a vast welter of things expressing absolutely nothing but cash value, jazzed up with scores of corrupt decorations plucked senselessly from their living contexts."

Above and right: The library of Chris O'Connell's Santa Fe house displays the rich variety of Native American art and represents many of the different tribes. The splendid Assinabo headdress hangs above a carved chief's bench from the northwest coast. The large pot is an Anasazi creation while the basket was made by the Pima tribe, who are famed for their basketry skills.

Left: Contrasting with the colour schemes of the Navajo weavings, the deep blues of the Chimayo rugs on the wall and sofa are particularly eye-catching. On the trunk is a Mexican drum and an Eskimo ivory ladle. Standard issue in every Santa Fe home, it seems, this particular kiva ladder is a very early example from about 1800. The design of the fireplace was based upon the Mesa Verde cliff dwellings in southern Colorado, the remarkable habitat of the early Pueblo Indians, where the vertical canyon walls of sandstone are punctuated with the jet-black rectangular openings that served as windows and doors to those dramatically situated homes. Below: The traditional Santa Fe ceiling of pine-log rafters was originally copied from Pueblo structures. Furniture in the dining room is early 1800s American, against which the Zuni and Zia pots are seen to best advantage. On the table is a Santa Domingo New Mexican dough bowl. Mexican crosses, candles and tinwork on the dresser sit happily with photographs of various Indian chiefs.

Since the 1920s, New Mexico, where the Native American culture is most firmly rooted, has attracted people fleeing from conventional society and seeking an alternative culture. Author D.H. Lawrence arrived at Taos in 1922, invited there by Mabel Dodge Sterne, a rich patroness of the arts, of whom Lawrence said she "hates the white world and loves the Indian out of hate". Mabel wanted Lawrence to see through her eyes, but to write in his hand "the truth about America: the false, new, external America in the east, and the true, primordial, undiscovered America that was preserved, living, in the Indian bloodstream". Although Lawrence at first found it difficult to relate to the Indians at all, he later wrote that: "Our darkest tissues are twisted in this old tribal experience, our warmest blood came out of the old tribal fire."

The type of house he lived in then, based on the Indian pueblo dwellings which Lawrence described as "like a pile of earth-coloured cube-boxes in a heap", has changed little and now stands as a perfect example of the "green" or natural house. In an environmentally conscious world, it offers valuable pointers, suggestions for ways to take up the most useful elements of a "natural" lifestyle in creating houses for the future.

On a fundamental level, the thick adobe walls act as passive solar heaters by absorbing the heat of the day and releasing it at night. The dirt floors have been replaced by natural alternatives such as brick or flagstone but ceilings maintain the same structure — wooden beams, over which are laid *latillas* or cedar striplings. In some houses, kitchen cupboards have fronts made from punched tin which keeps insects out while allowing the air to circulate inside. Corner fireplaces moulded out of sensuously curved walls add to the impression that these houses have grown naturally out of the environment; visually and psychologically, some even mirror the cliff dwellings inhabited by prehistoric Native Americans in southern Colorado.

Against the earth-like colours and textures of such a background, Native American artefacts such as the lustrous black Santa Clara Pueblo pottery or the richly coloured, graphically striped Navajo rugs are seen at their best. Items such as *kiva* ladders, used in ancient times for access to the special underground rooms known as *kiva*, have found a new lease of life in modern Native-American-look homes, often as a display frame for a vivid array of rugs.

When Spanish Colonial is added to the mixture, as in actor-decorator Thomas Callaway's house, a certain grandeur and glitter arrives with the more ornate furniture and chandeliers. But the Native American influence, with its strong colours and calm, natural framework, seems to bring the whole look down to earth, to stop it ever getting above itself. The end result is a pleasing balance, an assertion that the bedrock of Native American style is as firm and clear as ever.

Right: A stunning fireplace is created out of simple river rocks, as close to nature as you can get, and more impressive than the most exotic marble could ever be. The bleached skull, like the kiva *ladder, is more typically found in Santa Fe homes. Here the* kiva *ladder acts as a showcase for the Gubers' collection of Pendleton blankets. Native American artefacts are displayed on probably one of the wildest tables in the West: a glass slab supported by a tangle of antlers.*

Native American arts are at the height of their popularity now, as we have come to understand and empathize with the ecological philosophies of the North American Indians, which have reached the rest of the world too late. Different tribes have different strengths — most well known are the Navajo blankets, along with their silver and turquoise work, while Zia and Zuni make exquisite pots. Glass beads were introduced by white settlers, but the American Indians developed their own distinctive style of beadwork.

For the artist, the bohemian and the intellectual, Mexico has always held a fascinating, primitive allure. The writers D H Lawrence, Aldous Huxley and Somerset Maugham, and the patron of surrealist art Edward James are just a few of those who have felt its pull. Charles Macomb Flandrau, an American writing in 1908, linked its appeal to personality type. "A well-regulated, systematic and precise person always detests Mexico and can rarely bring himself to say a kind word about anything in it, including the scenery. But if one is not inclined to exaggerate the importance of exactitude and is perpetually interested in the casual, the florid and the problematic, Mexico is one long, carelessly written but absorbing romance." Other countries have the colour — the bright pinks, blues and yellows — but what sets Mexico apart is its frenetic quality, the feeling that underneath that sun-baked brilliance, the innocence of pure colour and the naivety of the child-like folk art, lie deeper, ancient passions. It is perhaps in the unresolved clash of a pagan civilization with the Roman Catholic Church, reverberations of which can still be felt throughout the nation's culture, that the clue lies to this land of dramatic intensity.

Left: Thick, rough-glazed, hand-painted crockery is the antidote to mass-produced uniformity and adds a haphazard gaiety and warmth to mealtimes.
Right: The decorative painter has borrowed traditional patterns to create a lively border at window height which adds native charm.

Above: Actor-decorator Thomas Callaway's Los Angeles house recreates the Spanish colonial atmosphere of Mexico — although scuffed painted cupboards and brightly coloured, thick earthenware pottery tip the decorative balance away from grand baroque toward a more modest, warmly welcoming peasant style.

Right: Traditional Mexican chairs set the ambiguous tone of grand primitivism, reinforced by the dark ambience of the paintings. The heavy wooden window frames and shutters, a feature of the house, were laboriously searched out in architectural salvage yards and garage sales. A wing chair upholstered in brightly coloured Navajo weaving lifts the room's predominantly brown tones.

Flandrau captured that fundamental flavour of Mexico when describing the interior of the cathedral in the town of Puebla. "The use of gold leaf in decoration", he wrote, "is like money. A little is pleasant, merely too much is vulgar; but a positively staggering amount of it seems to justify itself. . . . The ordinary white and gold drawing room done by the local upholsterer is atrociously vulgar, but the cathedral of Puebla is not. Gold — polished, glittering, shameless gold — blazes down and up and across at one." It was, he said, "one of those carefully insane 18th-century affairs, in which a frankly pagan *tiempolito*

and great lumps of Christian symbolism have become gloriously muddled for all time. . . . It isn't vulgar, it isn't even gaudy. It has surpassed all that and has entered into the realm of the bewildering — the flabbergastric."

The grafting of Spanish culture on to native Mexican life, which began with the invasion of conquistadors led by Hernán Cortés in the 16th century, had a profound effect on Mexican arts. The explosive combination of Spanish baroque and the natural Mexican exuberance led in the 18th century, for example, to a style of baroque more extravagantly expressive than anywhere else in the world. It would be wrong to presume that all the glitter and splendour was of Spanish origin. Cities like Tenochtitlan, as described by the 18th-century Jesuit Francisco Javier Clavijero, were hardly the work of a primitive people. "The houses of the rich", he wrote, "were of stone and lime with several tall chambers and great patios. The flat roofs were made of good wood, the walls were so well polished that the first Spaniards to see them thought they were made of silver. The floors were of mortar, perfectly levelled and polished."

Nowhere is the decorative impact of the meeting of pagan and Christian cultures more striking than in the Mexican celebration of death. The Day of the Dead, November 2, when people pay respects to their ancestors, is a Christian festival hijacked by pagan tone and colour as families set up altar-like tables in their houses, decorating them with fruits, flowers, candles and images of saints. The souls of the dead are said to be attracted to the colour and scent of the *cempasuchil*, the bright yellow "flowers of the dead", as well as to

Above: Fireplaces in the Callaway home are built in adobe style, their organic nature enhanced by the natural materials used throughout the house — the quarry floor tiles and wooden-framed windows and doors. Crucifixes may not be everybody's idea of tasteful decoration, used as a statement of style rather than religious belief, but there is no reason why they should not be appreciated in this context purely as works of art.

Left: A Spanish colonial theme pulls together the different elements of Tom Callaway's bedroom, where English pine and Victorian brass lamps are mixed with Navajo woven rugs, Native American dolls and a naive cowboy painting. The plank and beam ceiling structure is borrowed from traditional Spanish building techniques. Flaking paint on the French doors adds to the effect of age that pervades the house, even though much of it has been rebuilt. Callaway has most effectively upholstered a wing chair in Pendleton blanket.

Right: An adobe-style fireplace, stacked with Mexican tin, and above which hangs a painted tin and glass New Mexican cross, makes for cosy intimacy in a Santa Fe bathroom. Different ethnic styles — the round Swedish chair and Afghan wall-hanging — blend surprisingly harmoniously with the overall Mexican flavour of the decoration.

the copal incense which is burned before the offerings of bread, technicoloured foods and drink. Sometimes entire communities picnic on their loved ones' graves, while the shops are a riot of ornamental skeletons, bizarrely dressed in bright clothes. The skull symbol appeared throughout the Aztec civilization of ancient times, reflecting the constant concern with death; Mexican Christianity has merely clothed that fearful attraction in colour, giving morbidity a new hue.

But then this is the fascination of Mexican folk art — that underneath the apparent gaiety lies a thread of fatalism stretching back into the vaults of a deeply mysterious past. D H Lawrence evoked this darker side of Mexican culture in a description of the ruins of ancient Mitla in his much acclaimed Mexican novel, *The Plumed Serpent*: "the carved courts of Mitla, with a hard, sharp-angled, intricate fascination of fear and repellence".

The colours of Mexico are less calm than their Mediterranean equivalents — the pinks more brilliant, the blues more vivid, the yellows more acid, the greens more tropical. They are the colours of Mexico's

Thomas Callaway intriguingly combines the crudeness of thick Mexican pottery with the exotic decadence of religious ephemera. Elegant, highly polished furniture would look out of place — the sideboard has the well-worn ruggedness of much Mexican furniture; the chairs combine sturdiness with subtle ornamentation.

most famous woman artist, Frida Kahlo, whose unique home in Mexico City has inspired many a decorator worldwide.

They are also the inspiration behind the architecture of Luis Barragan, whose cement buildings succeed in capturing the spirit of adobe within the hard angles of modernity, the pinks and purples throbbing with the pulse of that deeper, darker underside that is the enigma of Mexican style. The basic style of ordinary Mexican houses that appealed to Barragan was recognized by Flandrau: "Whether the houses and buildings are built of stone or mortar or, as is customary in the smaller places. . . of sun-dried mud bricks, their effect is the same, for they are all given a coat of smooth stucco and then calcimined white, or a pale shade of pink, blue, yellow, buff, or green. . . and if it were not for their

gayety of colour, the perpetual fascination of their flower-filled patios. . . their uniform height and the square simplicity of their design might be monotonous."

Barragan was particularly influenced by the artist Chucho Reyes, who did much to awaken the people of Mexico to their own folk culture and turn them away from the French style of decoration which had become popular with the moneyed classes during the 1930s. The intuitively perceptive Reyes, according to Barragan, was "a great master in the difficult art of seeing with innocence".

Below left: The hall is given an ecclesiastical flavour by the Mexican religious painting.
Below right: A Spanish colonial santos *cupboard quietly dominates the living room.*

And difficult it certainly is. Interiors with a Mexican influence are in danger of appearing quaint if they ignore the rawer side of the culture. For instance, a collection of miniature, brightly painted Mexican figures, taken out of context and self-consciously lined up along a shelf in a prim room, has none of the attractive naivety or child-like natural sense of display that gives folk art its gusto. They need to be exhibited with the same sense of bravado and vitality in which they were created, perhaps set in an alcove of that wonderful bright matte blue, *azul anil*, which is traditionally used in Mexican houses for the purpose of warding off evil spirits.

Similarly, the temptation to use the ubiquitous elaborate beaten silver-tin mirrors as an inexpensive alternative to an ornate Louis-Quelqu'chose-style mirror in a plush

In Steve Weber's Santa Fe house, the kitchen manages to incorporate modernity within a Mexican framework. The soft curves of adobe walls offset the clean lines of the

kitchen cabinets, which are painted in that particular shade of Mexican blue known as azul anil. *An old table and chairs prevent it all looking too gleamingly new.*

The dining room achieves a strange, brooding calm — part ecclesiastical, part peasant and even part Gothic in flavour. Particularly effective is the elegant mismatch of old Mexican chairs. The use of sparse pieces of furniture against bare, natural surfaces gives an air of grandeur, which is softened by the primitive chandelier.

metropolitan, wall-to-wall-carpeted living room is too much for some to resist. But without doubt, neither will do the other any favours — the room will look too glitzy, the mirror too tawdry. To avoid such disappointment, the mirror needs to be appreciated for what it is, a vernacular craft piece, not a fake antique. It will work best when it is used with equally honest artefacts — such as the Mexican raw, unadorned wood furniture which has such a wonderful, chunky, anti-design simplicity to it and which is so blissfully inexpensive when compared with the over-refined, manufactured furniture found in department stores.

The basic materials of the interior need to be considered in the same light. There is nothing more visually uncomfortable than the primitive rubbing up against civilization in the form of wall-to-wall carpet and wallpaper. The key to successfully recreating Mexican style is first to build an appropriate framework of tiled or wooden floors and matte chalky walls, and then to fill it with, above all, a glorious riot of colour — colour, as Barragan put it, "for the sheer pleasure of using and enjoying it".

Above: The Webers' house was only recently built, designed by Santa Fe architect Bob Nestor. Yet with traditional building techniques and the incorporation of old fittings such as the hefty studded wooden doors, it has the spirit of a house that has been lived in and enjoyed for generations. Adobe-style walls often look best unadorned with pictures and decoration, but here where the three very architectural surfaces of slate, wood and plaster converge, the softening effect achieved by Native American and South American textiles works well. An array of American cowboy and baseball hats emphasizes the owners' eclectic and humorous approach to collecting.

Far right: Despite climatic and cultural differences, peasant style the world over has remarkable similarities. This painted Mexican cupboard in the Webers' bedroom could easily have been the work of a traditional Scandinavian craftsman from the point of view of both its colour and its style.

Right: The Webers have built up a large collection of primitive art from Mexico and South America, notable for its powerful religious and childlike naivety. Catacomb-like in its profusion of arches, this view takes in the kitchen with its traditional blue and white Mexican tiles.

Mexico's permanent sense of fiesta shines through in its crafts, bringing sunshine and colour to countries with grayer skies and less exuberant spirits. Mexican crafts, however, need to be displayed in the spirit in which they were made — over-indulgently. Gather masses of bright colour and tinware together: being half-hearted kills the spirit. Kitchens are particularly receptive to Mexican style.

The influence of climate on houses and interiors is at its most instructive in Europe. In the north, long hard winters keep the inhabitants housebound, encouraging a much cosier, more domestic form of home-making; in the south, boundaries between inside and out are more blurred and the house is less a refuge than a relaxed shelter into which to retreat from the hot summer sun.

But where similarities of climate lead to certain shared features, cultural differences result in variety. So although Scandinavian and Scottish ethnic houses might at first

Above: Tartan has a strong cultural and emotional significance for the Scots, but is enjoyed throughout the world for its warmth of pattern and colour; tartan designs are even used on ceramic dishes and pots.

Previous page: Interior designer Jacques Grange's Provence house is the perfect embodiment of relaxed Mediterranean style, unpretentious yet intuitively sophisticated. The coolness of natural stone, cream plasterwork, terracotta and metal is softened by the textural contrast of rugs and rushwork.

seem to have much in common — the box-bed built into the wall, for example, to keep out cold draughts — their differences are wider than the North Sea which divides them.

Although both were confined indoors for long winter months, the Scandinavians appear to have used their time more creatively than the Scots. Like the Poles and Russians, Swedish peasants whiled away the hours carving ornate wooden spoons, gingerbread moulds and spinning implements; Scottish wooden spoons, however, remained resolutely plain. Of course wood was a good deal scarcer in the Highlands and Islands than in Scandinavia, which doubtless affected whittling output, but beyond that there was a Calvinistic streak to the Scots which eschewed ornament per se. And the resulting strong, plain style has its own beauty. That the Scots loved bright colours can be judged by their tartan — perhaps no other nation has quite

Below: Box beds were a common feature of Northern European countries — this Swedish bedroom also squeezes in space for storage.

Below: Thick, rough-glazed pottery suits the robust and healthy Mediterranean appetite.

such a passionately romantic relationship with a fabric. But tartan also had strong military associations, and those probably overshadowed artistic considerations.

In Scandinavia and Eastern Europe the main focus was aesthetic. The Swedish were renowned weavers in Viking times, and have long favoured the more neutral colours that characterized Swedish textiles of the 1960s. But there were also splashes of colour — like the Russians, the Swedes had a passion for red embroidery. In both countries fringed and embroidered textiles hanging from beams softened the austerity of timber interiors. In Russia, the peasant carpenter's skills extended to barge boards, window shutters and balconies, all carved into a frenzy of fretwork and ornament, bearing witness to exquisite craftsmanship that must have lifted the spirit above the harsh realities of poverty.

The further south one goes, the less one finds ornate decoration. Mediterranean beauty, softened by the sun, is altogether more elemental. It relies on earthy textures and solid shapes — mellow weathered stone or sculptural whitewashed houses, their unblinking facades sealed with peeling green painted shutters. Inside are cool, tiled floors and whitewashed walls against which traditional French, Italian or Spanish furniture can be surprisingly dark and heavy. Interior comfort was never a priority in countries where much of the time would be spent in the fields or on the terrace.

Above: The warm earthy tones of large terracotta pots can be found throughout southern European countries, where terraces and courtyards play a central role in a largely outdoor way of life.
Left: Thick walls which keep out the heat in summer and preserve the warmth in winter have evolved as a natural response to the seasonal swings of the Mediterranean climate.
Below: Simple decorated boxes were often the work of peasants attempting to fill the long Scandinavian winter evenings. Originally, the simplest of rustic benches may have been the only form of seating in poorer Swedish and Scottish interiors, as in peasant homes throughout the Western world.

Even the designer-peasants of today who migrate to the Mediterranean areas of France and Italy shun the sophistication to which they might be accustomed in the city; chairs and sofas are covered in plain calico or in thick blue and white striped cotton, crudely painted rustic pottery replaces the elegant urban dinner service, and kitchens look as if the age of technology had yet to be invented. It's easy to dismiss all this as pretentious sham, but it is an almost instinctive response to the environment. In places like the South of France, any attempt to outshine those

materials that nature provides — the natural stone, the terracotta — will be disastrous: wallpaper, highly decorative textiles and luxurious furniture cannot compete. Perhaps it is not surprising then that taste has changed so little in the South of France since it first became a Mecca for artists and writers at the beginning of this century. All sought the same things there — not just the "delicious colour" noted by Vincent Van Gogh but a particular quality of life that could be found in the simplest pleasures. Their backdrop was the kind of interior described by Virginia Haggard, Marc Chagall's companion: "cool tiled floors and big tables spread with white cloths and crowded with heavy jars of mimosa and anemones. When the sun became hot and the green shutters were half closed, the light that filtered through them made everything glow like a Bonnard painting." It is a universal language of style that needs only the sun to translate it.

Above: Plain wooden furniture and warm natural tones, enlivened by decorative tiles, are the mainstay of European style.

A Celtic thread runs through Scottish culture, with its curiously opposing qualities of toughness and refinement; a warlike race, the Celts were also masters of exquisitely intricate metalwork. But superimposed on that Celtic heritage, it is the Scottish clan system, in which families banded together under hereditary chiefs for the purpose of mutual defence, that has done most to mould the character and culture of the Scottish people, engendering qualities of independence, hospitality and fidelity. Tartan is generally linked with the clan system, each clan claiming to have its own historic "sett" or pattern. It seems more likely, however, that the connection is relatively recent, and that in fact different regions wove their own particular tartans. A Skye writer, Martin Martin, wrote in 1703 that "every isle differs from each other in their fancy of making plaids as to the stripes in breadth and colour" thus enabling one "at first view of a man's plaid to guess the place of his residence". Whatever the rationale, highlanders have long been noted for their love of bright colours. Even Roman writers commented on the excellence of the colour and weaving of woollen cloth among the Celts in Scotland.

Left and right: The Stewarts' home is a designerly interpretation of Scottish vernacular, which combines honest materials — tongue and groove, seagrass matting and of course the national fabric — with a kind of homespun sophistication. They make especially free use of tartan, which is admired the world over for its warm, subtle colouring and design simplicity. The Orkney chair is a traditional design, its basket hood a cosy device to shelter the occupant from howling draughts around the back of the neck.

The early tartans of several centuries ago were simple checks of two or three colours obtained from dye-producing plants: blues from bilberries, greens from whin-bark or broom, yellow from bracken, while the muted brown colours desired for hunting tartans requiring camouflage were taken from lichens and seaweeds. Indigo and cochineal, prime sources of the favoured shades of blue and red, were imported from overseas.

For all its popularity, tartan was only invested with profound emotional significance after the wearing of it was banned in the Disarming Act of 1747 following the Battle of Culloden. Unfortunately, by the time the act was repealed 38 years later, many of the old weavers had died, taking

Left, below and above right: A clash of tartans — proof that you can't have too much of a good thing. Carpet, curtains, tiles and ceramics all sport a rich variety of checks and colour in a house that is essentially a modernized version of the traditional "but and ben" style. Having the cooking range in the living room may seem eccentric but it was considered a practical way of heating the living quarters.

their patterns with them. Nonetheless tartan underwent a great revival in 1822 when King George IV visited Edinburgh and suggested that guests attending the royal functions should wear their clan tartans. This resulted in a rash of creativity among weavers, as many a Scottish gentleman who found himself without a textile heritage decided to have an "ancestral" tartan invented.

In use, tartans were not necessarily restricted to clothing. The original belted plaid, six feet (1.8m) in width and 12 to 18 feet (3.7–5.5m) in length, would have been removed at night and used as a blanket, so usage in the home today as a throw or bedspread cannot be considered an inappropriate modern affectation.

The tendency in Scotland to apply craft to functional rather than artistic purposes relates to both the Scottish character and the environment that has helped to mould it. As writer Ian Finlay put it in 1948, the nurturing of a Raphael belongs to countries "where nature comes more than halfway to help the husbandman". Poverty and rugged living conditions concentrated skills on homey crafts rather than fine art,

Above: An 18th-century deerskin box on a 17th-century chest bears the unmistakable hallmark of tough Scottish craft.

so it was "natural in such a country that ornament should be functional, and that beauty when attained should be largely unconscious. . . . A certain ruggedness and vigour and bluntness of statement stand out as native qualities of special significance."

Certainly you don't see the "prettiness" in Scotland that you find in Scandinavian houses, although living conditions were quite similar. Evidently the Scots found something better to do with their long winter evenings than to sit around carving domestic utensils (perhaps the whisky had something do with it?) and yet there is something very pleasing about the austerity and honesty of Scottish interiors.

There were two basic styles of "peasant" houses. Most common were the obscurely named "but and ben" type, consisting of a living room and a sleeping compartment with earth floors. Sturdier in construction, the better-known croft, which went with a plot of land rented out to a smallholder,

was often built by the crofter himself and, as a response to the climate, had drystone walls of fortress-like proportions, plastered on the inside, with tiny windows. In some, known as blackhouses, there were no windows at all, the only natural light coming from the door and the smoke hole in the roof. Roofs were thatched — in the poorest regions using stubble or potato stalks, tied with heather or straw ropes fixed to stones.

Inside, the few pieces of native furniture have that beauty which comes from rational design: the Orkney chair, for example. This was made of a combination of straw and wood — originally driftwood, as there was hardly any local timber. Because of the scarcity of wood, the back was made of straw, and this soon evolved into a basketwork "hood" which sheltered occupants from the draughts that whistled through the windows on the galeswept island. The chair legs were always unusually short, so that the seated person was at a level below the smoke which drifted in the upper part of the room from the open fire in the centre, the only outlet being a hole in the roof — canopy chimneys were not common until the mid-19th century.

For everyday plates and vessels, pewter has always been a popular material. Finlay believed that there was "something in his nature which renders the Scot particularly suited to work with this austere material". There is not a great pottery tradition in Scotland, although the Isle of Lewis produced a type of peasant pottery, crudely formed and rather primitively fired by burning heather and seaweed, and of course there was Wemyss ware, a rather eccentric pottery with strong Scottish imagery. More recently Anta, a textiles

and ceramics company set up by Annie and Lachlan Stewart, has developed a range of tartan furnishings, including fabrics, floorcovering and tableware, which succeeds in capturing the rugged romance of the Celts and is rich in Scottish ethnic heritage, yet is at the same time distinctly modern. Annie strongly disavows nationalism but believes that, while the unification of Europe is having a standardizing effect on European countries, it is also helping them to emphasize their individuality. And Scotland, where an acute sense of colour combines with Calvinistic restraint, has a strong design statement to make. Tartan, of course, with its unique blend of outrageousness and classicism, will go on forever. It is, after all, Annie points out, the only fabric worn by both the Queen and punk rockers.

Right: In traditional Scottish interiors the bed was placed in a corner or, more commonly, built into the wall as a "box bed". Curtains were invaluable for keeping cold draughts at bay.

Below: Solid unpretentious furniture sits well with the down-to-earth comfort of Scots style.

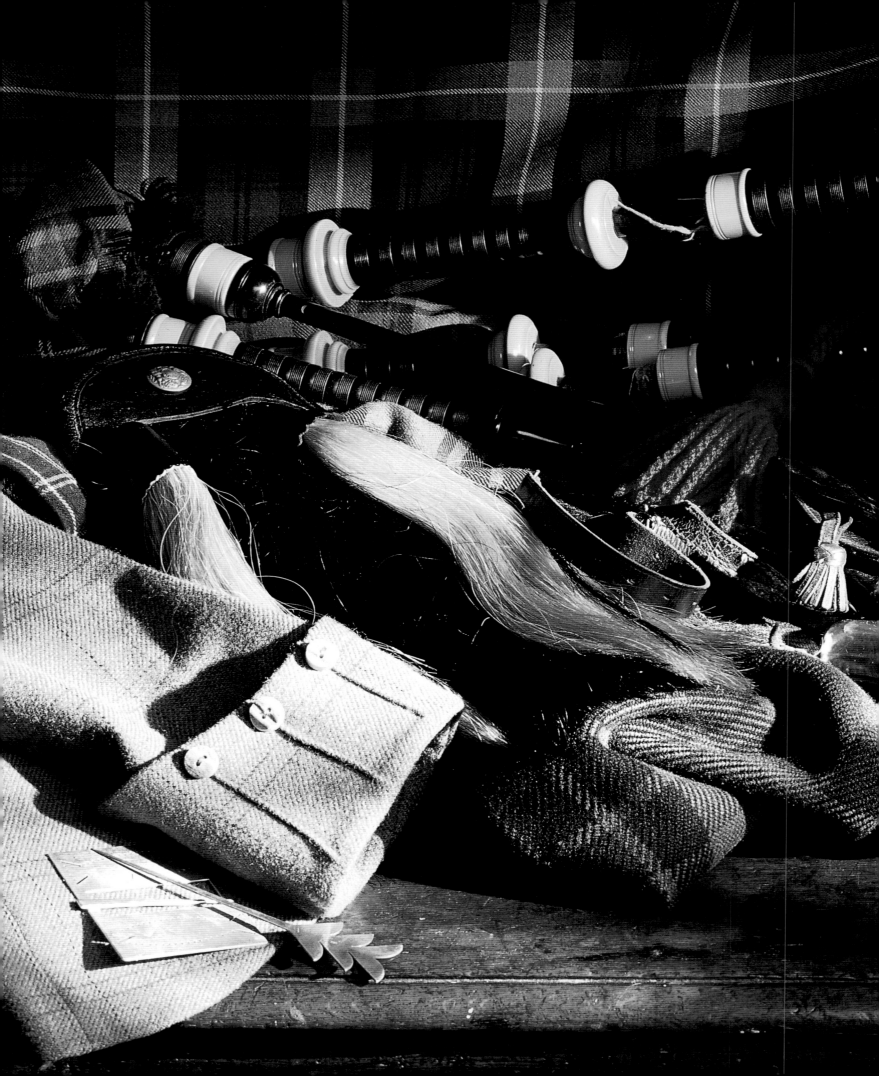

The raw materials of Scottish style are earthy and rugged reminders of a tough climate, landscape and history. But the macho effect of horn drinking vessels and leather deed boxes is softened by the romantic attachment so many Scots display toward their native instrument, the bagpipes, and tartan fabrics.

Long winters — sometimes lasting up to five months — have made their mark on the ethnic Swedish interior. For when the snow lay deep outside and there was little that could be done on the land, the peasant men took up their knives and planes while the women were busy at the loom. Often the ordinary household utensils such as mangling boards and spinning implements were exquisitely carved; disproportionately so, one might think, for such menial objects. But there was literally romance among the wooden spoons, for these carved objects in daily use — wood-*sloyd*, as they were known, *sloyd* meaning home-made — were lovers' gifts. When a young man was courting, he would set to work to *sloyd* a present which, if it was accepted, would show that the lady in question was likely to respond favourably to his advances. So, as writer Sten Granlund noted in 1910, "the twists and turns of the scutching-knife or mangling board are, therefore, emblematic of the tortuous dreamland ways along which the lover's thought wandered while he plied his knife." It was also traditional for a bride to present a bridegroom with an intricately embroidered linen shirt as a wedding gift, and the long task was often started well before a match was even on the horizon.

Left: In both child size and adult version, Swedish mid-19th-century chairs are simple but show a distinct design-consciousness in the carved detailing.

Right: This painted cupboard would have had pride of place in a Swedish farmer's kitchen in 1774 among the more severely utilitarian but honest hand-crafted chairs and trestle table.

Textiles were a primary source of interior decoration, the "indispensable handmaiden in the service of architecture", as Granlund put it, although the painted or woven hangings, with geometric or stylized floral motifs, were usually only brought out during wedding celebrations or at religious festivals. Plaited fringing, used to edge shelves and rafters, was a specialist craft often carried out by old women, who sold their skills from door to door.

Peasant furniture, at least until the aristocratic infatuation with French Rococo filtered through to more modest rural interiors in the 19th century, was generally plain and rather stocky. A primitive form of trestle table consisted of a wide board laid across two blocks of wood and hung on iron rings fixed to the wall when not in use. Utilitarian benches — known as *bäkbords bänken* (the bench along the wall) — were gradually replaced, in the interests of comfort, by chairs whose styles, even in remote villages, were copied from European examples. The truly indigenous chairs were a kind of tub chair made out of a hollowed tree trunk; the very organic-looking *kracken* stool, the legs of which

were formed from naturally forked branches; and the three-legged *blekinge* chair, which had a back and circular seat often made of plaited straw rope. On special occasions the seats would be covered with woven or embroidered cushions.

Sleeping places were usually of the "box-bed" variety, built into the wall and protected from draughts by curtains or shutters. Slightly wealthier housholds might also have had a curtained four-poster bed, from which hung a rope, twisted around with coloured yarn, that could be used for leverage by the old and sick. Every peasant household would contain a

Above: A central open stove was traditional to peasant houses — but they would have done without the luxury of a chimney. Simple gingham-covered Gustavian chairs and unpretentious furniture add to the homey atmosphere.

Above left: Although inevitably they vary in quality and degrees of ornamentation, tiled stoves and gingham fabric are common to both ethnic interiors and the grander Gustavian style of room — a democratization of style that could only happen in a country without rigid class barriers. The French-influenced 18th-century Gustavian style of furniture filtered through even to the most remote areas, inspiring peasant carpenters to be increasingly ambitious with their joinery techniques.

the symbol of light. They would also have one or two lanterns which featured horizontal rows of goose quills laid close together to filter the light — this charming kind of ersatz glass was sometimes used in windows too.

Inevitably in a country so heavily forested, timber has always been the main building material, and coping with a severe climate turned Swedes on to "green" design centuries before the rest of us stopped to think about the wisdom of squandering energy. Houses were always built to lie what is known as sol-ratt: with gable ends due east and west and the windows and doors facing south. Thick log walls acted as storage heaters, absorbing heat from the fireplace in the daytime and radiating it back at night when the temperature dropped outside, while on top of the birch bark roofs living turf acted as insulation.

Perhaps because times are now as hard in the West as the winters in Scandinavia, we have come to value the Swedish-style interior. After centuries of having eyes only for sophisticated decoration, we now have a new respect for their honest warmth that both uses and respects the environment.

Above: Woven runners were a practical and aesthetic addition to the bare floorboards of Swedish ethnic interiors; possibly it was Swedish immigrants who popularized the style in New England. Walls scraped down to the original paint flakes may look authentically rustic, but actually betray a nouveau-pauvre aesthete at work.

Above right: Box-beds — here in double-decker style, between them an elaborately carved and painted clock — were favoured in cold northern climes: woven curtains helped to ensure a peaceful, draught-free night. Long embroidered towels decorated the house on festive occasions. The rudimentary tub chair was one of the most ancient styles of peasant chair, easily created from a hollowed-out tree trunk.

chest, the making and decorating of which was a labour of love; in it were stored the linens, woven textiles and cushions. Corner cupboards and dressers were common, as were hanging shelves on which to display items that reflected the owner's status and wealth. There was also a special rack, or skedhyllan, for wooden spoons.

Lighting was usually supplied by the fireside glow, along with wooden torches stuck into iron wall sconces. But for festivals the Swedish peasants would bring out home-made candles, set in decorative candlesticks of wrought iron ornamented with bits of metal and often crowned by a cock,

Modern Swedish craft has retained the simple, homespun values of peasant production from centuries past, which marry very well with current designer minimalism. Wooden objects are left unadorned or painted in soft pastel shades, while gingham has lost its schoolgirl naivety and become a cool classic for upholstery and curtains or drapes.

Five hundred years of democracy and peace, Orson Welles remarked, and all Switzerland has to show for it is the cuckoo clock. Much the same attitude prevails among those who in recent years have developed a passion for Swedish and English peasant culture yet remain solidly impervious to the charms of Alpine or Tyrolean interiors. Perhaps it is the uncomfortable juxtaposition of cutsie cut-out hearts and heavy carved Gothic decoration — as the style has been interpreted by kitchen manufacturers — that has caused this aversion. Or perhaps it is because the rich and tasteless have made such a ghastly parody of it in their luxury Swiss chalets. Or could it be that we just can't take anything seriously if it comes from thigh-slapping lederhosen-wearers? Early this century, writer Clive Holland had a different perception of the Tyrolese. "It is not at all wonderful, then, that a people dwelling in a land of such surpassing beauty, where flower-bedecked upper pastures melt away into rocky peaks, glaciers and snow-clad heights. . . with the eternal silence. . . surrounding them and, as it were, shutting them in from the outer world, should be gifted with an appreciation of romantic beauty, legend and poetry beyond the common run of mortals."

Left: This kind of painted cupboard was common to peasant culture throughout Europe.
Right: Through mixing European peasant styles of furniture and accessories the Ventilos' kitchen evokes a mid-European/Tyrolean atmosphere that seems to meet the couple's own cultural mix — she is Swedish, he French — halfway.

Certainly the kind of reproduction painted peasant furniture seen today has no romance or poetry to it, but the cupboards and chests which survive from the 17th and 18th centuries show a level of artistic skill hard to match with notions of "primitive" peasant art. The more elaborate carved and painted pieces were executed by skilled craftsmen and formed part of a bride's dowry; her name and the date of the wedding were usually carved at the top of the bedhead or cupboard. As it was the custom to parade the dowry through the village streets, no doubt an element of "keeping up with the Joneses" crept into the lavish embellishment. Districts separated by mountains tended to develop local styles of carving and decoration — but very often, since Catholicism was so deeply ingrained, the subjects were religious.

Naturally, with the abundant supply of timber, most Alpine houses were built of pine, fir or larch wood, although those on a slope often had a stone substructure to keep the lowest floor at one level throughout. As for their cutsie ornamentation, according to Dr Franz Colleselli, an expert on Alpine and Tyrolean architecture, "everything about these houses has developed organically; every ornament has a purpose, and the way the wood is used shows how well craftsmen understood the properties of the material they were working in. These unassuming, functional buildings. . . reveal a high degree of artistic craftsmanship and a real feeling for rustic

beauty." The hearts and clover cut-outs, it turns out, are there for ventilation.

The heart of the Austrian and Swiss peasant house is the *Stube* or parlour. In some areas this was known as the *Rauchstube* (smoke room) and served as kitchen, living room and bedroom, smoke from the stove escaping through small, high windows. More common, however, was the *Ofenstube* (stove room) which, although it had a stove, suffered little grime or soot as the smoke escaped via the kitchen or an adjoining passage. Consequently the ceilings, unlike the smoke-blackened ones of the Rauchstube, were elaborately decorated. The *Stube* was the hub of the household. Here the family and farm workers took their meals and neighbours would gather to gossip on the bench around the stove. This wooden structure extended to a platform bed above, a warm, cosy place on cold winter nights. Originally furnishing was rough and basic — apart from the inevitable painted or carved wall-clock — but with time ornamental mouldings and decorative carving became an integral part of Alpine vernacular. Pride of place went to the chest, made at first by peasants themselves for storing corn, later by craftsmen for linen and clothing.

Sadly, however, as elsewhere, with industrialization the peasants started to look down on their own traditional and artistic handiwork. Many beautiful pieces were relegated to attics or outbuildings, perhaps to be unearthed in the 1950s when connoisseurs were beginning to recognize their value, and the trend for *Bauernstube* — living rooms decorated in peasant style — took hold of those who were, in terms of income and lifestyle, furthest removed from peasant status.

Left: The wood-panelled bedroom has a cosy Alpine feel, emphasized by the patchwork hanging. The heart motif is common in Tyrolean woodwork — and what more appropriate place for it than a bed?

Left: Copper pans hanging from wooden beams and a simple lace-edged valance at the window alert us to the presence of designer-peasants.

Right: Objects from different ethnic sources can be successfully mixed, sharing as they do similar motifs and symbols. The fireplace is the focal point of the room, as was the stove in a traditional Alpine home.

Below: After religious scenes and representations of the four seasons, floral painting was the most commonly found decoration on Alpine furniture. This kind of work would probably have been carried out by a travelling artist.

The heart dominates Tyrolean craft — it can be found on everything from houses to chairs and chopping boards. Cross-stitch embroidery shows a marked resemblance to Eastern European handicraft, although floral embroidery has its own distinctively Alpine appearance. Gingham fabric provides a simple background for such decorative detail.

Peasant culture is a hardy plant. Despite the twin blights of progress and affluence, still it manages to flower in pockets of Russia, Poland and the East European countries. In 1912, the author of an article in *The Studio* magazine bemoaned the fact that conditions in the Ukraine had "dulled the inborn artistic instinct of the Ukrainians. . . . As a result we see here. . . the general decline of the true peasant art, and the substituting for it of factory-made ugliness." Princess Tenisheva attempted to reverse this trend in the increasingly industrialized Russia of 1893 when she established her estate at Talashkino as a centre for the revival and promotion of folk art. But sadly, most of its natural creators — Polish women who made *wycinanki* (intricate paper cut-out designs), Russian peasants who carved or painted even the most basic of household utensils, from wooden spoons to gingerbread moulds — did not appreciate the value of their own work. Inevitably, they came to view their home-made creations as inferior to expensive machine-made goods. Peasant crafts implied peasant status. Even now, folk art is a sophisticated taste, so anyone travelling in Eastern Europe will usually be proudly shown by enthusiastic locals the ultimate in 1960s plastic.

Left: Painted eggs, originating from Easter celebrations, are common to many East European countries, most strikingly displayed piled together in a myriad of colour and pattern.
Right: The window alcove in artist Barbara Dorf's tiny kitchen is crammed with objects culled from her travels, but the composition bears the imprint of an artist's hand.

But where examples do still exist, the general style of the interior has hardly changed from the last century. In the mountainous regions of Poland and the wooded areas of Russia, timber is the dominant material. Everything from the *izba* (Russian peasant cottage) to furniture, toys and utensils is made from wood — the Russian people, wrote the collector Princess Alexandre Sidamon-Eristoff in 1912, "are carpenters by instinct". In a few remote areas of Russia, the kind of interior she described then may still be found. "The simple furniture consists of seats, either fixed or moveable, a few tables, a sideboard for the display of plates and dishes, and some chests embellished with metalwork or painting. The peasants delight to decorate the undersides of the lids of these coffers with popular engravings. . . . In the right-hand corner of the wall, called the *krasni ugol* (beautiful corner), are placed one or more holy images or icons before which wax tapers or little oil lamps burn, forming a family altar. Sometimes there are a few engravings either of religious subjects or representing popular heroes, a loom for weaving, and a few household objects."

Artist Barbara Dorf has made her London kitchen into a complete *krasni ugol*. The daughter of a Russian mother who left in 1905, she inherited some of her Slavic collection from relations but has added Polish, Russian and Yugoslavian artefacts and textiles gathered on her travels. There are friezes made from strips of Russian cloth ("printed, I'm afraid; originally they would have been woven or embroidered"), wooden and lacquer plates painted with fat flowers, bowls full of painted Easter eggs, Russian lacquerware, bright painted

enamel saucepans, paper flowers, decorated wooden spoons, icons, Polish cut-out paper designs. . . all jammed together in a glorious cacophony of colour.

Here is the same abundance of spirit that has always characterized Eastern European peasant interiors, often in contrast to the rigour of their lifestyles. "The excellence of external form, the beauty of cardinal lines do not constitute the aesthetic value

Left: In Slavonic homes embroidered hangings were only displayed on festive occasions; at other times they were stored in the household chest. Barbara Dorf, however, inspired by stencil designer Carolyn Warrender's work, has used them as permanent friezes all round the walls and doors. Traditional Slavonic lace (also above) is used to edge the shelves, and the cloth of lace-edged squares on the dresser was inherited from her Russian mother. Mixing colour and pattern together with abandon like this was common in peasant households.

of peasant production," wrote Maryan Wawrzeniecki in *The Studio* magazine in 1912. "The harmony and even the discordancy of colour, these are the true tokens of peasant art."

Barbara Dorf does not dismiss the tourist production of peasant craft, believing that it is better than it dying out altogether. In a robust collection like hers, the occasional Russian tourist-shop wooden doll or bowl is simply another element of the colour carousel. But there is no doubt that such pieces lack the depth and warmth of those objects that were made with love and used with appreciation.

Textiles are an important part of Eastern European interiors: in Russia special embroidered towels and *chirinkas* (squares of fabric) were made by the women as wedding gifts and draped from the beams in the *krasni ugol*. Red was the most common colour used for their cross-stitch embroidery: an old northern Lithuanian proverb says "What is red is beautiful," and indeed in the Russian language "krasni" can mean both red and beautiful.

A peculiar characteristic of Polish peasant interiors, which can still be seen in the area of the Tatra Mountains, is the treatment of pillows. These are piled up or laid side by side, as many as six or seven, at the foot of a bed. Like the embroidered towels of Russia, they are wedding gifts, made from precious goose down collected over the years and stuffed into elaborately hand-worked cases. They are valued both for the work that goes into them and for the scarcity of the down filling, taken from the breast of the goose. How empty in comparison seem the status symbols and achievement markers of the "civilized" West — the television and the three-piece suite.

Russian craftwork is distinguished by its highly lacquered decorative paintwork. Much of the work produced for the tourist trade is lacking in the original peasant charm, but the bright colours — if used en masse, and without trying to be too sophisticated about coordination — are some compensation. If in doubt, pile it on. . . .

The word Mediterranean instantly evokes a certain quality of light and of colour that fuses together the essence of France, Italy, Spain and Greece. But the heart of Mediterranean style lies in Provence, fed over the centuries by so many different cultures. The area was first colonized by the Greeks, then invaded by Celts; later it became the first Roman province outside Italy, coming under Spanish influence in the 12th century and then returning to Italian domination in the next century when the papacy established itself at Avignon. The 18th-century historian J-P Papon described Provence as the "garden of the Hesperides, which under a beautiful sky produces the perfumes of Arabia, the riches of the Orient, Spain and Africa". Artists who colonized it later in the 19th and early 20th centuries found it fertile territory for their work. "The future of modern art lies in the South of France," wrote Vincent Van Gogh in 1888 — and

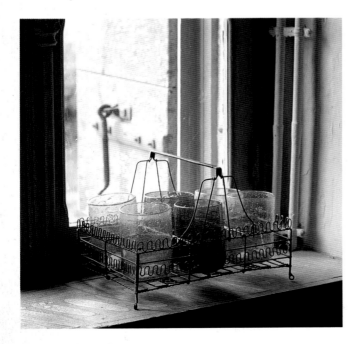

the list of artists who lived and worked there at some point reads like an index to modern art: Claude Monet, Paul Cézanne, Auguste Renoir, Henri Matisse, André Derain, Maurice de Vlaminck, Raoul Dufy, Pablo Picasso, Fernand Léger, Georges Rouault, Georges Braque, Marc Chagall. . . .

Left: Ornamental wirework, a traditional craft of France, is enjoying a revival: functional objects such as wine-bottle crates take on a new aesthetic role when filled with coloured glass.
Right: Kitchens throughout the Mediterranean have an attractive earthiness, with terracotta and stone floors, beamed ceilings and thick, roughly glazed pottery tableware.

Left: The mellow tones of a stone fireplace and a mass of pots orchestrate the Provençal theme in designer Jacques Grange's home.
Top and middle right: The Mediterranean look is cooler than its Asiatic or African counterparts, but influences from India and North Africa are evident.
Bottom right: The sun motif of Fornasetti's chair is apt in Provence, where the poet Mistral wrote of souleiado (the sun's rays piercing the clouds).

The writer Ford Madox Ford described Provence as a "highway along which travelled continually the stream of the arts, of thought, of the traditions of life". In a letter to his brother Van Gogh explained why the South of France was so conducive to creativity. "Although the people here are blankly ignorant about painting in general, they are much more artistic than in the north in their own persons and in their manner of life. I have seen here figures quite as beautiful as those of Goya or Velasquez. They will pin a touch of rose on a black frock, or devise a garment of white, yellow and rose, or else blue and yellow, in which there is nothing to be altered from the artistic point of view."

But above all it was colour, brought to life by the special clarity of light, that fed his senses — and that epitomized the flavour of the Mediterranean. A still-life such as he described could be found on a table in Provence even today: "a coffee pot in blue enamel, a cup on the left, royal blue and gold, a milk jug in squares of pale blue and white; a cup on the right of white with a blue-and-orange pattern on an earthen plate of grayish-yellow; a jug in earthenware, or majolica, blue with a pattern in reds, greens and browns; and lastly two oranges and three lemons."

Above: Natural tones and rough plaster walls are the essence of Mediterranean spirit.

Colour and texture are the riches of Mediterranean life, based on simple pleasures and available materials: terracotta, basketry and ironwork. Van Gogh perceptively noted that homes were "less dreary and less dramatic than in the north since the warmth makes poverty less harsh and melancholy". The poverty may have disappeared, at least in the South of France, but the simplicity that it engendered remains.

Indeed, affluent interiors seem completely out of place in the Mediterranean. Rich fabrics and exotic furniture look tawdry when asked to compete with sunshine, hence the dominance of plain cream calico fabrics or simple checks and stripes for upholstery and the solid, unpretentious wooden furniture that has ruled the Mediterranean roost for centuries. The armoire has long been the mainstay of every French household — a large cupboard used to store both food and clothes, it was embellished with carved decoration if the family were wealthy

enough to employ the skills of a craftsman. Every kitchen traditionally would also have hanging from the wall a *panetière*, a box for bread, often carved with religious imagery — appropriately enough, given the French devotion to their daily bread. But the basic make-up of the kitchen is the same whether in France, Italy or Spain: a tiled or flagged floor, rush-seated wooden chairs and a solid pine or oak table indented with the memories of meals enjoyed and shared over the years.

Design, too much carefully laid detail, is anathema to a Mediterranean interior. Parisian interior designer Jacques Grange has certainly felt no need to stamp his profession all over his Provençal house: the interior makes no demands on its occupants other than to relax and enjoy. The metal bull sculpture might seem to add inappropriately Spanish overtones, but in fact bull-fighting (a rather more humane version than that practised in Spain) was once an important part of Provençal life. Frédéric Mistral, 19th-century writer and champion of Provençal culture, said that "in the south the passion for bull-fighting is more deeply rooted than in Spain itself."

A relaxed charm that shuns pretension, colours that take their cue from nature — there is the essence of Mediterranean style. Van Gogh expressed the feelings of thousands of others after him when he wrote that he wanted to make his little yellow house with green shutters truly "an artist's house — nothing precious, but with character in everything from the chairs to the pictures".

Right: The rusticity of massive bleached beams is balanced by cool contemporary furnishings.

Against a background palette of earthy tones and textures, the decorative work of the Mediterranean countries shines through, whether it is in the Islamic intricacy of Turkish tiles, the kaleidoscopic brilliance of Provençal prints, or the rough, painterly verve of thick Tuscan pottery.

Above: Tribal beads are displayed against the dull glow of golden metallic walls, evoking the hot dusty atmosphere of Africa.

For centuries Africa was the Dark Continent — mysterious, uncharted, untamed. Of only one thing were Europeans sure: it must contain an inferior civilization with an inferior culture. When, in the late 19th century, explorers penetrated the interior and found traces of ruined cities and exquisitely worked gold jewellery, they declared it to be evidence of a vanished white people, believing that no black peoples could have built such a civilization.

It was not until 1897, when the Royal Navy brought back to Britain bronze castings and ivory carvings seized in reparation for losses in Benin, that an appreciation of African craft began to develop. But the

Previous page: Interior decorator David Champion's home is a skilful blend of Western design and detailing with African imagery and colour schemes, transporting an ordinary city house to the realms of intriguingly distant exotica.

first Europeans really to recognize the intense vitality and spiritual power of African art were the Fauvist and Cubist artists, through whom it had an explosive impact on Western art. "We attribute a rudimentary taste to the savage who is delighted by glass beads," wrote Albert Gleizes and Jean Metzinger in their essay on Cubism in 1912, "but we might with infinitely greater justice consider as a savage the so-called civilized man who, for example, can appreciate nothing but Italian painting or Louis XV furniture."

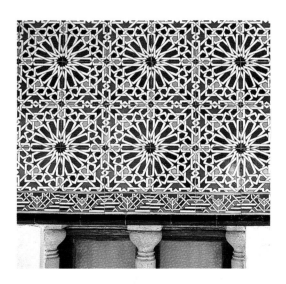

Above: The strong Islamic influence on North Africa can be seen in the intricacy of tiles and windows.
Right: Embroidered sackcloth curtains strike the right note of improvised splendour.

Only in recent years is the same impact being felt in decorative and applied arts. Dr David Livingstone spoke of the Makololo being amazed by machine-printed cottons from Manchester, "so wonderful that the Makololo could not believe them to be the work of mortal hands" — which, of

course, they were not. But today we look with the same amazement at Africa: at the fast-disappearing areas where cloth is woven by hand on double-heddle looms, where plants and river mud still yield up their colours, where design is as unselfconscious as breathing, and patterns seem to be plucked from the communal subconscious. Africa is too often conveniently packaged as a land of mud huts and tribal masks. But of course in such a vast continent, with widely differing terrains, from rainforest through savannah to arid expanses of desert, there are huge cultural variations. North Africa, with its Arab influences, is a far country indeed from the grasslands of South Africa. While accessibility opened the north, and also the Gold and Ivory Coasts, to trade and external influences, the interior remained for a long time closed to Western values and concepts. Architecturally, the styles of houses are as various as the building materials to hand, but what links them is the African sensitivity to texture and pattern — be it the intricate filigree work of a wooden shutter against the bright blue of a Moroccan wall or the magnificent "pop art" walls of an

Above: Tribal masks are not restricted to wood. This beaded embroidery elephant-mask in cotton was made in West Africa.

change, declaring "the old native dwellings . . . infinitely more picturesque and their native ornaments. . . infinitely more interesting than the awful 'Brummagem' atrocities sold to them by the traders".

Even the squalor of urban poverty cannot entirely kill the creative spirit of Africa — its ghost still struggles to express itself in the ramshackle townships of South Africa. The indomitable urge on the part of the Ndebele and Basuto people to create, to beautify, has survived the indignity of being uprooted from their traditional villages: corrugated iron roofs are pasted inside with a collage of magazine pages, while shelves which traditionally would have been edged with a clay frill are given scalloped borders cut from magazines.

This adaptability, the ability artistically to

Above: African sculpture was the inspirational force behind new creative trends in Western art at the beginning of this century.

Ndebele mud house, painted with a mixture of acrylic paints and colours taken from the earth. For Africans in traditional rural areas it is not enough simply to build a roof over their heads; their homes express both themselves and the sculptural qualities of mud. Decoration is applied in a variety of ways: scratching abstract patterns with fingers or forks, perhaps pressing millet and maize cobs into the damp mud. The tradition of embedding china and brightly decorated enamel plates into the mud, to frame a doorway or window, has its origins in the 15th century, spreading across from East Africa. Often the plates are smashed, forming a kind of ersatz mosaic.

It is this almost childlike lack of inhibition — still much in evidence, although rapidly being quashed by invading Western culture — that is so precious. As early as 1903 an English visitor to Africa, Minnie Martin, recognized the danger-signals of

Above: Decorative treatments are applied to all aspects of African living. Calabashes or gourds were carved into geometric patterns and used as containers or drinking vessels.
Right: Egypt is generally considered separately from the rest of the continent and remembered only for its ancient culture, even in modern interpretations.

ad lib, is what gives African style its verve and suggests that although traditions may change they will never be extinguished. But the wealth of creative expression seems to go hand in hand with poverty, and we cannot expect Africans to deny themselves escape from that simply to give us the pleasure of enjoying something we ourselves lost long ago.

To
day North Africa is a favoured hunting ground for designers: irresistibly drawn, they come to seek inspiration in that cross-fertilization of two cultures, Moorish and African, which gives the region its special exotic flavour. In the 19th and early 20th centuries, however, it was not designers but artists who staked their claim on these lands — **Eugène Delacroix** and **Henri Matisse** in Morocco, **Paul Klee** in Tunisia. **Delacroix**'s visit to Morocco in **1832** provided a wealth of Orientalist imagery for his paintings, but it is interesting that he needed to distance himself before its influence could be used to greatest effect. Twenty years after his North African experience he declared in his diary: "I began making something passing out of my trip to Africa only after I had forgotten all the little details and in my pictures retained only the striking and poetic side. Until then I had been pursued by the love of exactness, which most people mistake for truth." The same philosophy applies equally well to design. Painfully trying to recreate another country in your living room after ransacking the souks on a two-week tour results in at best a turgid realism, at worst a conglomeration of lifeless kitsch. But when the interest goes deeper, success is much more likely.

Left: The "casbah" interpretation of North Africa piles on the colour.
Right: Interior designer François Gilles's apartment in London conjures up a cooler, French colonial vision of Morocco. Exotic furnishings such as the screen and the zebra-skin rug are used with typical designerly restraint.

*Above: The walk-in cupboard off the bedroom has an Arabian Nights allure
with its old chenille drapes and Moroccan rug.*

*Left: In designing his bathroom Gilles was determined to create the kind of sense of
sybaritic luxury that can be found in the grandest Moroccan hotels, a place redolent
of perfumed oils and baths of asses' milk — although again it is very much the
designerly interpretation of Arabic style. The walls are naked plaster, finished
where they meet the ceiling with a leather trim more normally used to edge library
shelves. As a skirting or baseboard device he has chosen English tiles in a simple
but striking Moroccan design.*

Personal motivation is the key to the London home of French interior designer François Gilles, for whom Morocco has a particular significance. For the French, the love affair with North Africa is very much the same as the British with India, a sentiment undoubtedly rooted in their colonial pasts. Gilles's grandfather had made several trips to Morocco before finally leaving his family to go and live as a painter in the desert there. The influence of those early visits could be seen in the Moroccan-style drawing room of their family home on an island off the coast of Brittany. Gilles has vivid childhood memories of the dark green woodwork and exotic feel of that room — memories which have been re-awakened by his own recent encounters with Morocco and which he has tried to encapsulate in the decoration of his London apartment. But it is recreating not so much through objects as through feeling.

What appeals to Gilles is the idea of something being rough and refined at the same time, the way the Moroccans "do things simply but with wonderful gesture — the comfort of sitting on cushions, eating couscous with your fingers". His bedroom and alcove bathroom are wonderfully sensual and indulgent, yet at the same time have a kind of primitive feel that comes from the pink cement walls, simply finished with a matte varnish. (In Morocco, points out Gilles, the dull sheen to the walls is obtained by rubbing down with pieces of marble.) He had trouble persuading his London builders to make the rough arch-shaped openings into the bathroom

Above left and above: In contrast to the cool elegance in the rooms beyond the heavy studded doors, Gilles has made a small, intimate sitting room, emphasizing the den-like atmosphere with the use of a palm wall-covering normally found in mosques. The Arabic motif on the cushions is echoed in Gilles's own designs.

Right: Traditional Arabic decorative motifs also feature on the mirror. Antique markets provide good hunting grounds for curios like the zebra-foot lamp.

120

less than perfect, but it was necessary to avoid the association with manicured suburban lounges, in which the archway is seen at its weakest — an inappropriate gesture toward exoticism.

Gilles's home is a perfect example of accommodating North African inspiration without denying a Western framework. The living area is in a thick, light-reflecting cream, very much the typical elegant high-ceilinged 19th-century London apartment, yet it is unmistakably the home of a Frenchman. The plaster lightshades with cut-out shapes were designed by Gilles and made for him by a sculptor, so they are decidedly modern and yet the way in which they cast shadows and play with the light recalls the latticework and intricacy of Islamic art. Huge double doors, decorated with black metal studs, are reminiscent of Morocco but can also be seen on the grander portals of London and Paris — it is this kind of

Above and right: You can't go wrong if you go completely over the top when it comes to the Moroccan tented look. West Coast interior decorator Sandra Sakata has built up a huge collection of ethnic furniture, jewellery and textiles which she uses to dramatic effect.

Above: Intricate decoration, making elegant use of classic motifs, frames a glass-fronted wooden bookcase in Parisienne Françoise Lafon's Egyptian suite. The North African theme is echoed in the mirror above.
Left: Extravagant in its decoration and yet understated in its colour scheme, the Egyptian bedroom with its late-19th-century Orientalist spirit arose out of interior designer Jacques Grange's discovery of some Egyptian boiseries, which had been salvaged from a private theatre.
Below right: Echoing the Orientalist theme in its early-20th-century mirrors and stained glass windows, the bathroom, with its plump rounded bath and soft smudged walls, has an aura of decadent luxury.

domestic equivalent of some of the more garish Orientalist paintings of the 19th century must be the "old hippy" interior with its tented ceilings, joss sticks and brass pots filled with dried grasses. In order to avoid artistic colonialism, says Schneider, "the foreign land must cease to appear foreign and seem as familiar to the painter as the Seine at Argenteuil seemed to Manet or the Montaigne Saint-Victoire did to Cézanne."

A sensitive approach is especially important when it comes to Egyptian artefacts, where there is an enormous gulf between creative contemporary craftsmanship and mass-produced representation of ancient splendours. Early Egypt's prosperity and sophisticated civilization had much to do with geographical advantage — the Greek historian Herodotus called Egypt "the gift of the Nile". For as the Nile burst its banks once a year, and then receded again, it left large fields for cultivation and animal rearing. The resultant food surplus supported craftsmen such as weavers and metalsmiths, while at the top end of the social scale the kings or pharoahs boasted enormous political power and wealth.

cross-cultural reference that makes the whole place work so homogeneously.

Of course, one of the great attractions of North Africa is its exoticism, but if you take that alone and out of context — like scraping the icing off the cake — you are often left with a rather tawdry glamour. Exoticism in painting has been described by Pierre Schneider, when writing about the painter Henri Matisse in Morocco, as the artistic version of colonialism. This could equally apply to interior design: the

Naturally, people nowadays look at the huge advances made in early Egyptian civilization and wonder what happened, that it should now be relegated to Third World division. But of course the hieroglyphics were only open to priests and scribes, and the amazing architectural calculations were implemented only for building pyramids and temples — the type of mud-and-thatch hut that the ordinary Egyptian lived in can still be seen today. Because knowledge and power were invested in such tightly defined social groupings, progress eventually stagnated.

The pinnacles of past achievement are reflected today in the miniature pyramids and pharoah's heads that parade as Egyptian "art" in the tourist shops. However, the discerning collector need not despair — there is still plenty of genuine ethnic art that does not need to feed off the glories of ancient history: a strong tradition of metalwork, combined with Islamic influences, for example, results in wonderful brass globe lights with cut-out star shapes and balls of coloured glass. In Cairo's largest bazaar, the Khan al-Khalili — a warren of tiny, medieval streets and passages where shops sell spices and scents, fine Muski glass beakers and jewel-bright recycled glassware — craftsmen practise the ancient crafts that have not changed over hundreds of years. Egypt is where Asia meets Africa, with all the creative vigour typical of hybrid cultures around the globe.

Whichever element of North African ethnic art you choose, colour needs to be imported with care. It was in Tunisia that the artist Paul Klee claimed to have discovered it, while in Morocco Henri Matisse declared that he "felt the passion for colour develop in me"; and Charles-Edouard Le Corbusier's inspiration for his white architecture supposedly came from early visits to North Africa. But there is a difference between letting the colours of another country stimulate your palate and simply regurgitating them without reference to climate or culture. The pinks of Tunisia, the blues and greens of Morocco, which look so vibrant under a clear blue sky, can be tawdry and depressing in the gray light of northern climes. Yet applied with intuition, a North African effect can be magical indeed.

Left: Zaza Van Hulle creates a Moorish extravaganza in her Paris apartment. Floor cushions, huge brass trays set on wooden stands, Moroccan-style banquettes, a ceiling fan, filigree brass lanterns and a jungle of towering plants conjure up an atmosphere far from temperate urban reality. Just sink back into the pillows, take a sip of aromatic tea, and imagine the desert heat beating down outside. . . . Below: The bathroom is an Odeonesque fantasy of Moorish delight. When Zaza Van Hulle moved into the apartment she discovered the columns and arches underneath a thin partition of plaster; given her love of travel, they posed an irresistible invitation to her escapist decorative schemes.

Right: Evidence of a global shopper is stacked along the shelves — colourful exotica and dark carved wood are both seen to best advantage against the mint-green of the drawing-room walls. The brightly coloured throw over the sofa is an exquisite example of Cameroon appliqué work; the leather cushion is Moroccan, while those beside the sofa are covered with Ghanaian kente fabric.

Below: Curvaceous cream chairs and sofas lend the drawing room the air of a 1930s Moroccan hotel, despite the wide variety of ethnic artefacts and fabrics from all over the globe. The black and white check carpet, echoed elsewhere in the apartment in linoleum, provides a graphic background for the colourful ethnic textile throws on the furniture, and the 1950s glass table cuts through the clutter. Archways and pillars, fundamental to Moorish architecture, dramatize the atmosphere of a cool, cavernous interior.

Above: A romantic painting of camels and palm trees, together with the guide book below, shows where the owner's heart lies. The collection of ethnic objects works surprisingly well visually despite their widely different origins.

North Africa is quite distinct from the rest of the
continent — the Islamic influence is clear in the
intricate, non-figurative patterns of the thick pottery
and the silk and wool rug. From Egypt comes the
tactile pleasure of thick recycled glass in a range of
bright, bubbly colours.

Africa activates the senses like nowhere else on earth. Its colours and smells are so vivid that the visitor carries them around long after he or she has left African soil, as if somehow the very essence of the country has got under the skin. That "hot sweet smell of the land", mused the British writer Graham Greene — what was it? " . . . the starved greenery and the red soil, the bougainvillea, the smoke from the huts . . . or the fires in the bush clearing the ground for planting? It will always be to me the smell of Africa, and Africa will always be the Africa of the Victorian atlas, the blank unexplored continent the shape of the human heart." French novelist André Gide wrote evocatively of the air which "blows sometimes so light, so suave, so voluptuously soft, that one seems to be breathing deliciousness." That deliciousness extends to African crafts. Between high art — the rare carving, which English critic Margaret Trowell described in the 1930s as "combining the force of a good carving by Epstein with the fineness and delicacy of work strongly reminiscent of the best carvings from the Egyptian tombs", and tourist tat — lie the everyday objects dignified by decoration from the heart.

Left: Brightly coloured bowls made from telephone wire show the African ability to adapt ancient traditions to new methods — in the past these artefacts relied on natural materials.
Right: In his choice of colour scheme, decorator David Champion intuitively celebrates the colours of his South African homeland — black, yellow-gold and green. On the mantelpiece he mixes modern Western pots in jewel-encrusted pewter with old African grain pestles and figures by African potter Hylton Nel.

Primal passions, unfettered creativity — it's easy to understand the excitement caused by African art when it was first "discovered" by artists at the beginning of the 20th century. The French Fauvist painter Maurice de Vlaminck was given a Fang mask in 1905 which revealed to him "all the primitive grandeur of African art"; when his fellow Fauvist painter André Derain saw it he was so overwhelmed that he bought it from Vlaminck and showed it to Pablo Picasso and Henri Matisse; Ambroise Vollard then borrowed it and had it cast in bronze. The French painter Georges Braque told how "the Negro masks. . . opened a new horizon to me," and in 1922 the Spanish Cubist painter Juan Gris decorated his apartment with a cardboard copy of a Gabon funerary figure. The vitality of an art uninhibited by rules of representation and imbued with symbolism encouraged Western artists to break open their traditions of painting and swept a new spirit of freedom through 20th-century art. Even the most avant-garde movements seem to have precursors in Africa — you can see Op-art in BaSongye masks and the American artist Keith Haring's graffiti style in walls decorated by Ndebele women, while today's Western textile designers strive hard to capture the wonderful graphic simplicity found in appliqué cloth from Dahomey or the instinctual design sense so apparent in indigo resist-dyed *adire* textiles that are produced in Nigeria.

Calabashes — hardened gourd shells made into bowls, drinking vessels and containers — highlight the African impulse to beautify. Easy to obtain and prized by nomadic tribes in particular for their portability, their value increases on decoration. As Frenchman René Gardi wrote in 1969, "millet, peanuts or milk can be preserved just as well in an undecorated calabash as

Left: David Champion's sitting room displays the same mannered arrangement of art and design as the vestibule on page 131. Although the overall influence is African, other ethnic pieces don't intrude on the style. Thai temple dogs, stripped and repainted by Champion, guard the fireplace while the hearth is tiled in modern English encaustic tiles decorated with ethnically inspired motifs.

Below left: On the mantelpiece an African "basket" jug made from painted bottle tops is filled with porcupine quills. Their spikiness is reflected in Champion's choice of plants throughout the house — tongue-like leaves and tall grasses shoot out of vases, giving a hard-edged virility to the design.
Below: The abstract cushions are made from mud-resist Mali fabric.

A lustrous gold for the walls was achieved with metallic paint normally used on radiators. The giant coloured cardboard and rattan basket was created by Lois Walpole, the artwork on the wall by Champion's eight-year-old daughter Ida, using African river mud, ochre oxide and Reckitts blue.

in a decorated one. But in a land where people are not yet so obsessed with functionalism the decoration of the object is not regarded as a superfluity that yields nothing, but rather as a necessity and a chance for self-expression." In some areas the ornamentation is burnt into the gourd skin with hot knives, in others it is carved or engraved; but always the patterns — linear, geometric and spiral — are applied freehand, as if the maker is guided by a kind of innate aesthetic drive. Of course it is a dying craft: plastic and enamel bowls are more durable and easier to wash.

Calabashes are still being decorated, but they are bound for the tourist market, and somehow — like the masks carved in traditional ways but without the original spiritual purpose behind their creation — the patterns seem to have lost their intrinsic rhythm and vitality.

Taken in isolation, as decorative objects divorced from the spirit in which they were made, African art can be depressing. A row of ebony figures set on built-in teak shelving in some stifling, carpeted room invokes nothing of Africa, nor does the self-conscious minimalistic posing of masks

art. "Painting is in my heart," explained an Ndebele woman to American photographer Margaret Cameron Clarke. "As long as I am able to paint, then I will carry on this tradition."

In a culture where creativity is a necessary form of self-expression, the ability to accommodate new materials is impressive, especially as even the most hermetic and soulless are imbued with a wholesome verve. One of the most potent examples is the use of coloured telephone wire to make bowls once crafted from sorghum grass: what started with a few bored night-watchmen "borrowing" new materials that came to hand has now become a bona-fide craft, with a huge demand from the designer shops of the West.

This instant designer status, however, is slightly worrying: the trade is good for the Africans, but will gratifying the West in terms of colour and pattern suppress their own cultural instincts? Wherever tourists tread, a self-parodying ethnic style or "airport art" can be found, but to have Western trends guiding the maker's hand is potentially very damaging — particularly when, having exhausted "ethnic" as the current fashion story, the West pulls out. African objects look best arrayed selectively in a sympathetic environment, although this need not be taken to extremes; there is something rather ridiculous about the mud-hut-in-Manhattan syndrome. David Champion's rooms are crammed with objects, but there is a sense of aesthetic order, and the mixture of African pots and "fetish" sculptures along with commissioned pieces from Western designers and craftsmen is highly effective. Undiluted ethnic — widely practised in the 1970s — can be hard to digest: the ability to edit is crucial.

Above: In the dining room the ecologically correct ebonized ash dresser with worked copper inserts, designed by Champion and his partner Anthony Collett, displays African baskets and Afghan pottery. Right: The table and chairs are original Arts and Crafts pieces by Ambrose Heal, perhaps the ultimate in vernacular English but their solid craftsmanship fits surprisingly well with the crude vitality of ethnic items. Champion is an insatiable patron of modern art and craft, always attracted to the same primitive exuberance found in African art. The rug in the foreground is by Linda Hampson, who normally works in woven calico in the Greek tradition but was commissioned by Champion to make this piece, incorporating raffia and seagrass in an African mode.

in a designer-white setting, like trophies from a global shopping trip.

In contrast, London interior decorator David Champion's home is an instinctive journey back to the South Africa he grew up in: the golden ochres and reds of his drawing room are a reminder of the earth from which the tribespeople used to take pigments to paint their houses. Even now, the Ndebele and Basuto people mix acrylic paints with browns and ochres from the earth, white from slaked lime and black from used batteries, just as tribal iconography has been adapted to incorporate light bulbs, bicycles and skyscrapers into their

Tribal Africa, an impenetrable mystery to the Western world until the 19th century, has a wealth of treasure to offer the intrepid buyer who can see beyond the shiny superficiality of tourist art. Rough woven textiles, the smooth tactility of age-worn wood, and beadwork which avoids "prettiness" are all to be found in tribal art.

"The sun was reflected, with a glare scarcely more supportable than the heat, from the massy gold ornaments, which glistened in every direction. . . . The *caboceers* [chiefs], as did their superior captains and attendants, wore Ashantee clothes of extravagant price. . . . They were of incredible size and weight, and thrown over the shoulder exactly like a Roman toga; a small silk fillet generally encircled their temples, and massy gold necklaces, intricately wrought; suspended Moorish charms. . . a band of gold and beads encircled the knee. . . manillas and rude lumps of rock gold hung from their left wrists, which were so heavily laden as to be supported on the head of one of their handsomest boys. Gold and silver pipes and canes dazzled the eye in every direction. Wolves and rams' heads as large as life, cast in gold, were suspended from their gold-handled swords." Such was the sight which overwhelmed Thomas Bowditch when he was sent

from Britain in 1817 on a diplomatic mission to the kingdom of Asante (now Ghana) to increase the gold trade. Visiting the Gold Coast a few years earlier, Henry Meredith, reporting back to the African Institute in 1811, was less impressed. "The country is not distinguished with Eastern splendour; art is scarcely known in it," he declared.

Left: Nuristani chest and African chairs marry surprisingly well together.
Right: Huge beams like raw tree trunks support the structure of Judy Bergsma's home, whose original owner, textile designer Jack Lenor Larsen, wanted it to have the feel of Bantu architecture. The "bird" sculpture is from the West African Senufo tribe.

It is only recently that we have come to appreciate the applied arts of this area of Africa. Meredith did not consider textiles to be an art, yet to the Asante the wearing of fine cloths was a mark of status and privilege, valued almost as highly as gold. The Asante are best known for their *kente* cloths, *kente* being a Fante word meaning basket. Once the prerogative of the king, *kente* cloth is now commonly worn by Ghanaians on formal occasions. The cloths are made from narrow strips of woven fabric, sewn together in a dazzling basket-work effect of intricate pattern and colour. There are three basic categories of textile, from the simplest stripe, *ahwepan*, to the most complicated and evocatively named pattern of all, *adwineasa*, meaning "my skill is exhausted".

Ever since trading began, the Africans have made skilful use of European and Asian cloths, unravelling silk to use in their own designs, or adapting them by over-printing or pulling out threads to create new patterns. An anecdote from the Kuba people of Zaire, famous for their textile patterns, tells how, presented with a motorcycle in the 1920s, their king was apparently unmoved by the machine itself but fascinated by the tyre marks which it left in the sand. The pattern was promptly added to the Kuba collection.

The West Africans also built creatively on necessity. The appliqué technique often seen on raffia dance skirts features a kind of comma-shaped motif known as "the tail of a dog". It is thought that this was originally simply a patch used to repair tears until its decorative potential was spotted.

As well as weaving, the Asante also produce stunning printed fabrics known as *adinkra*. These are made using printing

Above: Studded Moroccan doors lead through to a bedroom, which has the cool, spartan feel common to North African and Mediterranean sleeping quarters. The natural, almost dilapidated wood of the doors contrasts well with the smooth white walls — gloss-painted studded doors, as seen in London or Paris, have a grandness to them which would distort the balance designer Christophe Decarpentrie has succeeded in achieving between comfortable elegance and austere ethnic.

Left: White walls and dark furniture is the domestic picture that the Gold and Ivory Coasts conjure up. British colonials who returned from Africa brought the style with them, but managed to invest it with a particularly unattractive Victorian gloom. Decarpentrie uses it with more success in his Brussels home, adding grandly eccentric touches such as the antler chandelier. The carved intricacy of the door frame is not normally associated with Africa, but in fact in towns around the Gold Coast area, such as Djenne, marvellously ornate architectural decoration can be seen in abundance. On the whole, however, the tropical lifestyle and philosophy seem more at home with a rougher, largely symbolic style.

stamps cut from small pieces of calabash or by drawing wooden combs dipped in ink across the fabric.

In Nigeria, the Hausa and Yoruba people have made particular use of resist-dye techniques. The Hausa city of Kano had about 2,000 dye pits in the mid-19th century: obtaining indigo from indigo leaves was a complicated procedure left to specialist craftsmen, but the more common colours were easily and generally available to spinners and weavers — yellow from turmeric or brimstone bark, brown from certain tree barks, black from river mud, and red from the camwood tree or henna. Several methods of resist-dyeing were used. Patterns were sometimes painted on freehand with starch or applied through stencils cut from thin sheets of roofing zinc, in which case the design would only appear on one side of the cloth. For a less precise pattern, the cloth could be tied or folded and sewn with raffia. The Yoruba often made *adire* (resist-dyed) cloth by sewing or tying sticks, stones or seeds into the fabric before dyeing.

Besides their *kente* cloths and gold-casting (paralleled by the lost-wax bronze casting of Benin), the Asante have traditionally made fine stools. Stools were more than just a functional object — they were felt to be linked with the owner's personality and status, some of the more elaborate designs, such as those in which the seat is supported by a leopard or elephant, being reserved for royal behinds.

Everyday stools used by the lowest ranks in society are known as *nkonnua fufuo*, or white stools, because they were regularly scrubbed with water and fine sand, and occasionally lime juice, which gave them a clean, white colour. The Asante were obsessed with hygiene and cleanliness, which was felt to be particularly important for something like a stool so closely associated with the person who owned it. Occasionally a white stool was converted to the important status of blackened ancestral stool (*nkonnua tuntum*). Only an office-holder who was judged to have led a successful and blameless life was deemed worthy of having his stool blackened, a process involving soot, raw egg and the blood and fat of a sheep. When this delightful mixture congealed and darkened, the stool would be left with a shiny, black seal. It was then kept with other ancestral stools in a special room in the palace which was considered sacred and could only be entered by the most senior people.

Perhaps the most telling point about Asante stools lies in the contrast with the much grander-looking chairs that they also made. Apparently based on 17th-century European designs, these were not invested with the same spiritual significance as the simple stool. And that was what Meredith could not see: European work may display fine craftsmanship, but African designs combine that with heart and soul.

Right: Sunlight brings to life the dark tones of the living room, softening the hard textures of tile and matting. There is nothing cosy about this interpretation of ethnic — it is stern and imposing, a fit setting for the nobility of the African pieces, like the carved column with inlaid Islamic brass script and the ad-hoc table, which now groans under the weight of books but once graced a camel's hump.

Below: Many Western textile designers take inspiration from ethnic traditions: the fabric covering the sofa is a modern interpretation of Kuba cut-pile raffia textiles from Zaire.

Much of the appeal of classic African folk art lies in
its abstract pattern. The wall hangings could be a
modern fabric design, yet they are in fact 19th-
century Kuba palm-fibre appliquéd skirts from Zaire
— stunning thrown over a sofa or used as hangings
for wall or windows. Good African carving is difficult
to find. Old pieces, such as this Guro mask from the
Ivory Coast, are rare and expensive, while recent
work is all too often cheap tourist fodder made from
machine-tooled ebony. On the other hand, modern
clay pots and baskets have lost none of their integrity:
the two-tiered pot with scarification markings is a
contemporary Nigerian creation.

Tradition is a living thing in Asian countries. In Europe or America it is something to be preserved in museums, brought out and admired occasionally but kept strictly in the past — a measure by which to judge how much we have progressed. To be traditional is considered boring, unadventurous, uncreative.

Yet even in Japan, the most technologically advanced country in the world, tradition is not just alive, it breathes life into the future, co-existing with progress in healthy symbiosis. In Indonesia the patterns used in batik and *ikat* fabrics have not changed for hundreds of years and yet they have a vitality and freshness that somehow still

Previous page: Textile designer Jack Lenor Larsen applies Japanese principles of ordered design to big-city living, echoing textures of stone and wood in fabric and carpeting. Sliding screens act as room dividers without eating into the space, while raised platforms provide under-floor storage.

Above: Appliqué work from Jaisalmer complements a Bombay colonial bench.

Above: A Chinese New Year arrangement of plum blossom and tulips is set against a 1920s Tibetan vegetable-dye rug; nowadays these are largely produced by Tibetan communities based outside their homeland, in Northern India and Nepal.
Below right: The effect of Japanese rice paper, too fragile for a Western lifestyle, can be achieved by using sand-blasted glass.

carries the creative spirit of past generations — at least when made by hand, for even here the machine marches on in invincible fashion, plundering authenticity and tearing out its soul.

Bamboo has left its mark on the houses and interiors of many Asian countries. In Indonesia it is used for floors and walls, in Japan and India for water vessels and shelves. American Edward Morse, who wrote about Japanese houses of the 19th century, described and sketched a bamboo rack for cooking implements — a piece of bamboo with "pockets" cut into it at regular intervals to hold wooden spoons and so on fixed to a wooden post — that could have come from an elegant designer store of the 1990s.

Looking at the skill of craftsmanship in Asia — the wood carving of India and Japan, the weaving of Indonesia — it is clear that all the sophisticated tools and machinery of the West, while they may save time, have not taken us any further; indeed in terms of craft they may have held us back. Edward Morse compared the American carpenter's "ponderous tool-chests. . . filled to repletion with several hundred dollars' worth of highly polished and elaborate machine-made implements" with the Japanese carpenter's "ridiculously light and flimsy tool-box containing a meagre assortment of rude and primitive tools" and concluded that "civilization and modern appliances count as nothing unless accompanied with a moiety of brains and some little taste and wit."

In part the superiority of craftsmanship is

due to attitude. What is considered to be the 20th-century British builder's disease — "can't be done, guv" — was evidently rampant in the last century too. Morse contrasted the United States with Japan, where he was amazed to see "how

leaves in Sumatra, elephant grass in Bali or, in Japan, a grass called *kaya* — although the fire risk has almost eliminated thatch there in favour of shingle. Traditionally Japanese roofs featured an ornamental motif just below the ridge tiles; often this would be a relief of foaming waves, possibly because a watery subject was felt to protect against the danger of fire.

Religion permeates the cultural life of Asia. Even the shape of the houses, generally airy wooden structures with overhanging roofs, is largely Buddhist-inspired, a celebration of the tree under which Buddha found enlightenment. Where Islam made converts there can be found the most intricate non-figurative patterns and decoration, although Indians largely tended to overlook the Islamic stricture forbidding depiction of humans or animals — considered tantamount to playing God — and consequently many of their patterns combined the richness of Islamic decoration

patiently a Japanese carpenter or cabinetmaker will struggle over plans, not only drawn in ways new and strange to him, but of objects equally new — and struggle successfully." In America, however, he complained, "most of the carpenters in our smaller towns and villages are utterly incompetent to carry out any special demand made upon them, outside the building of the conventional two-storied house and ordinary roof." And in Bali today, the most primitive forms of housebuilding often conceal a comparatively sophisticated technology.

Throughout Asia the roof receives great attention, the elaborateness of its decoration often quite disproportionate to the simplicity of the rest of the house. Generally roofs are steeply pitched, both to repel rainwater and to shade the verandah. In Indonesia, religion and superstition govern the decoration: the gables of Batak houses are often crowned with carved buffalo heads, while Sumatran Minangkabau houses are an extraordinary sight with their profusion of spiky gables.

Thatch is the most common roofing material, made from palm fibre or pandanus

Left: Paisley, which has taken the name of the Scottish town whose weavers copied it from Indian designs in the 19th century, originated in Kashmir. Below: Traditional Japanese design philosophy, increasingly rare in the Far East, has been enthusiastically adopted by Western minimalist designers as a statement of modernity.

with the liveliness of their own. In India the elaborate painting inside temples has been imitated in houses, and the blurring of cultural and religious traditions may go some way toward explaining the popularity of the huge, hand-painted film posters that dominate urban streets — and often the remotest of rural bedrooms. In Japan the sense of order, pattern and harmony at the heart of Zen Buddhist philosophy can be seen in the calm of a raked gravel garden or the immaculate order of a minimalist interior, designed to promote contemplation. Today religion is very much alive in some parts of Asia, while in other regions it has been superseded by an altogether more cynical materialism. But throughout the continent, its influence continues in a rich heritage of living arts.

Below: The eclectic glitter and gaudiness of India provides inspirational source material for Western fashion and graphic design.

To understand the Japanese home, it helps to understand the Japanese. Perhaps no one was better at explaining both than the American observer Edward S Morse, who wrote *Japanese Homes and Their Surroundings* in 1886. The traditional house, although now few and far between, has changed little since then: it is based on a way of living prescribed by Zen Buddhism, governed by *shibui* — a word which has no direct translation in English but conveys the idea of simplicity, restraint and understatement. To the Westerner, the first sight of a Japanese house can be disappointing. Its gray-brown, rain-stained boards can appear drab, and classical interiors are almost empty — no fireplace, no mantelpiece, no furniture and no rooms as such. Instead of windows there are *shoji*, wooden gridded frames covered in rice paper; more solid screens called *fusuma* act as moveable partitions between rooms. For the average Westerner the lack of

privacy might be intolerable, but then it could be argued, as Morse so succinctly put it, that "privacy is only necessary in the midst of vulgar and impertinent people — a class of which Japan has the minimum, and the so-called civilized races — the English and American particularly — have the maximum".

Left: Steel-hard modern minimalism marries well with the traditional Japanese sense of order in fashion designer Issey Miyake's kitchen.

Right: Such rigorous minimalism, even in the bedroom, requires an equally rigorous, unslovenly lifestyle — razor-sharp hospital bed corners absolutely mandatory. . . .

Above and right: Opaque screens or fusuma *glide open to reveal part of Jack Lenor Larsen's collection of metalwork and ethnic textiles. The fabric half-curtain, known as a* noren, *which is suspended above the door is more traditionally used in shop and restaurant entrances in its native land.*

Interiors follow the same principles in every traditional house, using the same basic materials and with the same respect for simplicity, whether the owner is rich or poor. *Tatami* mats cover the floor, providing a comfortable, tensile surface for the bare foot. They are made from a pad of compressed rice straw, about two inches (5cm) thick, covered with a taut matting of woven *igusa* reeds, the edges bound in a tape of black linen or bright brocade; each mat measures six feet by three feet (1.8m by 0.9m). So fundamental to the Japanese way of life were *tatami* mats, as bed, table and chair, that they became a unit of measurement, still standard even for modern apartments today. Added to the aesthetic qualities of this calm expanse of pale honey colour, broken only by the graphic lines of the edging, *tatami* is thought to

restore oxygen to the air of a room. Even so, sadly most Japanese nowadays prefer wooden flooring or even Western-style carpet, although many keep at least one *tatami* room in their apartment or house, usually as a bedroom.

Together with the smell of the natural wood used in the basic construction of houses, the light, airy qualities of *tatami* flooring compare very favourably with the average stuffy Western room. Certainly after enjoying "the fresh air and broad flood of light" of Japanese homes, Edward Morse found it hard to enthuse about the typical American interior — "encumbered with chairs, bureaus, tables, bedsteads, washstands, etc, and. . . the dusty carpets and suffocating wallpaper, hot with some frantic design".

Traditionally the interior space of a Japanese house has two recesses. One, called the *tokonoma*, is empty except for perhaps a picture or scroll and a vase containing a branch of cherry or plum blossom. This is the place of honour, in front of which guests are seated. Only one item is displayed at a time so that it can be fully appreciated: one object of beauty inspires peaceful contemplation, it is reasoned, whereas too many things over-stimulate. Although times are changing, the cluttered bric-a-brac of Western rooms would, in Morse's day, have driven the Japanese frantic. They, he wrote, "have never developed the miserly spirit of hoarding truck and rubbish with the idea that some day it may come into use."

The other recess, the *chigai-dana*, contains a closet and shelves, concealed behind sliding doors. Essential items, such as the futon mattresses which are folded up during the day, are usually stored here.

With these recesses, as elsewhere in the house, symmetry is scrupulously avoided. In direct contrast to the Western perception (beauty for us tends to mean symmetry: the central mantelpiece, with its ornamental centrepiece flanked by matching candlesticks), the Japanese find aesthetic satisfaction in asymmetry.

One of the strongest influences on the arts in Japan has been the tea ceremony, with its rigid simplicity and the mannered rusticity of implements used: the tea ceremony is one way of promoting the sought-after state of *wabi*, or "finding satisfaction in poverty". In particular its effect can be seen in Japanese pottery — the rough texture of Raku and stoneware which had such enormous impact on leading Western potters like Bernard Leach. Morse had a theory that, in a happier parallel to the effect of Calvinism on early Puritans, the Japanese tea house "suppressed the exuberance of an art-loving people, and brought many of their decorative impulses down to a restful purity and simplicity."

It is this same spirit that sees beauty in what Westerners might regard as rather drab colours; where a Mexican or Caribbean is exhilarated by bright pinks and blues, a Japanese is moved by carefully neutral colours and the subtlety of differences between them. Plaster walls inside the houses Morse described were given slight variations of colour and texture by the addition to the plaster of tiny gray and white pebbles, pounded shells or even fibres of finely chopped hemp.

Tradition and uniformity can so easily be boring — as in Western suburbia — but in Japan they are not. The spiritual purpose and sensitivity to detail create a subtly controlled naturalness and lift design above mundanity.

Above: More commonly covered with rice paper, screens are also an effective way of using the many pretty translucent fabrics which tend not to get hung in Western windows because they never quite lost the "net curtain" stigma. In the traditional Japanese home futons are rolled away in cupboards when not in use, but Larsen prefers the permanence of a sleeping platform hidden behind screens and a thicker, softer mattress and pillows rather than the extra-firm variety usual in Japan.

Above left: The effect of seeing accumulated treasures all at once is regarded by the Japanese as the visual equivalent of overeating: fusuma *serve as a way to ration helpings of Lenor Larsen's collection of pottery, sculpture, paintings and photographs.*

Jack Lenor Larsen's collection of hats and baskets reflects his extensive travels throughout the Far East in search of inspiration for his textile designs, but the basic layout and detail of the interior structure of his New York apartment is specifically Japanese in feel, particularly in his use of blond woods at ceiling height to define spaces. There is also a Japanese emphasis on quiet, peaceful colours; the gray-green walls are typical.

After centuries of trade isolation, Japanese artefacts have been adopted with great enthusiasm by the West — perhaps focusing more on their decorative than functional roles, as the delicacy of Japanese cups and bowls requires a gentility of appetite that does not come easily to the average Westerner. Old textiles are highly sought after, particularly for their exquisite range of indigo blues.

At the heart of Indian ethnic culture lies colour — vibrant, spicy, pulsating, clashing, gaudy colour. "Pink", said Diana Vreeland, the late Voice of Fashion, "is the navy blue of India." Even in the midst of the most grinding poverty, there is richness of colour, whether in the glittering saris which appear like mirages in the dusty desert landscape of Rajasthan or in the lurid film posters towering above the urban squalor of Calcutta. To reach the true essence of India, you have to dig beneath the cultural overlay of colonialism. The image of heavy, dark wooden furniture in white-walled rooms that we associate with India is the legacy of the British in India, a gloomy reinterpretation of Victorian Surrey which evokes at a glance that depressing, chilly feeling of being inside a sunless room on a bright, sunny day. In fact the Indians didn't possess furniture until the English came along and made them feel undressed without it. From peasant houses to palaces, the favoured form of seating was the floor. Other cultural invasions have been more beneficial. Mughal rule left some fine architecture, while in Kashmir conversion to Islam in the 14th century was the catalyst for an exceptional flowering in the decorative arts, stimulated by craftsmen from other Muslim countries.

Left: The delicacy of Indian carving forms a perfect contrast to the solidity of ancient wood and studded metal straps. The table displays a selection of punched brass ladles, pots and bangles.
Right: A dealer in West Rajasthan artefacts, David Wainwright's London home shows intricate workmanship in the late-18th-century Goan cupboard and the mirror made from an old window.

During the 18th century Kashmir became famous for its finely woven teardrop-pattern shawls, known quite unfairly to posterity as paisley, after the Scottish town whose weavers managed to create much cheaper imitations of the shawl that for 70 years or so had captured the hearts — and purses — of European women. The weaving was so fine that one shawl could take up to six months to make; but when all and sundry started sporting cheap paisley lookalikes, not even the finest workmanship and highest prices could convince the haute monde to continue patronizing Kashmir. In 1877 famine finished off what fickle fashion had started:

Right: The table was originally a magistrate's desk, its imposing height intended to put defendants squarely in their place.
Below: A temple cupboard from 1830 is set on wheels because of the weight of teak.

Above and left: Designer Steve Wright's apartment captures the frenetic brilliance of India within a framework of esoteric designer-iconoclasm. The walls are created through a hectic build-up of paint, his own design wrapping paper and collaged images of religious and pop idols.

the Kashmir weavers were wiped out, and with them died their skills. An original Kashmir shawl is both rare and valuable — and so too now is an old paisley; time has given it the status it lacked.

Like the other crafts of India, embroidery is restricted to traditional patterns and techniques and yet never looks tired or dull. Increasingly Western buyers are using the skills of Indian needlewomen for their own designs to make exquisitely embroidered sheets, pillows and cushions — but not, it is to be hoped, at the expense of traditional techniques, such as Kashmiri crewel-work. Crewel-work is a type of chain-stitch embroidery, thickly worked in wool on cotton, now regaining popularity in the West as curtain or drapery material. Woollen chain stitch, coarse yet immensely expressive, is also used on felt to make rugs called *numdah*. *Gabba*, another Kashmiri floor covering, are made from thick woollen cloth — sometimes old blankets — cut out and stitched on top of each other in intricate appliqué work. Apparently the 19th-century Sikh leader Ranjit Singh was so pleased with one he had ordered that he threw himself on the floor and rolled himself up in it.

If all clients were so enthusiastic about craftsmanship, perhaps many of the skills of India would not now be losing their integrity and dying out. But then this was starting to happen as long ago as 1895. Sir Walter Lawrence, a British civil servant, wrote that "Papier mâché has perhaps suffered more than any other industry from the taste of foreigners. . . . Ask an old artist in papier mâché to show the work which formerly went to Kabul and he will show something very different from the miserable trash which is now sold. But the Pathans of Kabul paid the price of good work; the visitors to the valley want cheap work and they get it."

Peasant housing varies in India according to climate and terrain. In the northern province of Kutch, where the hot dry season gives way to monsoon rains, the circular mud and dung houses are built on platforms to protect them from flooding. But hard living never obviates the need for decoration. Inside walls and cupboards made from the same mud and cow-dung mixture are incised with a pattern made by the women using their fingertips, and then whitewashed — lending unbelievable exoticism to such very basic materials. Common in many peasant households is a curious fabric-covered bulge: this contains the dowry sheets — each daughter is expected to make at least 15 — piled up on a stool or small table and then covered over with cloth. Beds are either the basic Indian rope-sprung *charpoy* or a simple bedroll which is put away in the daytime. Often the poorest areas are the most richly decorated, as if to compensate for the material deprivation with visual food. The mud-brick walls of Rajasthan houses are enlivened with silver trinkets suspended above the doorway and primitive reliefs are composed of shards of coloured glass and mirror. Red handprints on the outside walls are not just a decorative motif — they signify the birth of a son. Thus colour and creativity take on a key symbolic role in the richness of Indian decor.

Below: Culture vulture and magpie are both at work in Wright's creations: boxes and mirrors encrusted with jewels and buttons frame images of film idols.

Indian style swerves between exotic brilliance — the sumptuousness of jewel-coloured silks, the intricate designs of exquisitely painted papier mâché and finely worked brass — and the unadorned beauty of elemental, rough-hewn wood and basic metal bowls and boxes. Most types of Indian crafts are readily available, be they the cheap and cheerful trinketry from import shops or the more dignified antiques to be found at specialist dealers.

Bamboo is the design currency of Southeast Asia, the staple material of living in Indonesia, the Philippines, Malaysia. . . . It is, wrote natural historian Alfred Russel Wallace in 1869 in *The Malay Archipelago*, "one of the most wonderful and most beautiful productions of the tropics, and one of nature's most valuable gifts to uncivilized man". Sadly, we in the West tend not to see it at its best in the typical creaky bamboo couch, bought only for economy and looking depressingly out of place on wall-to-wall carpet. In Indonesia bamboo is used in ways which exploit its practicality and enhance its beauty, as Wallace found in the Dayak houses of Borneo: "The floor is always formed of strips split from large bamboos, so that each may be nearly flat and about three inches [8cm] wide, and these are firmly tied down with rattan to the joists beneath. When well made, this is a delightful floor to walk upon barefooted, the rounded surfaces of the bamboo being very smooth and agreeable to the feet, while at the same time affording a firm hold. But, what is more important, they form with a mat over them an excellent bed, the elasticity of the bamboo and its rounded surface being far superior to a more rigid and a flatter floor."

Left and right: San Franciscan interior decorator Sandra Sakata brings together a harmonious mixture of furniture, textiles and accessories from the Far East, balancing slender bamboo pieces with the heavy opulence of polished wood. Korean trunks in the foreground, right, display Chinese and Thai wooden bowls. Afghanistan is represented on the chaise.

A tablescape captures the drama of Eastern style. Against the backdrop of an antique Japanese screen, the rich vibrancy of fruit and exotic flowers highlights the dark exoticism of a mask from Bhutan set on a Thai bowl. The grapes are placed on a Japanese stand, the apples in a wooden bowl from Tibet. Covering the table, a textile from Laos pulls the different elements together.

Above: An antique bureau displays a sumptuous collection of Eastern exotica, presided over by the superbly detailed Japanese Boys' Day figure of the general Yoshitsune, symbol of manly strength; nowadays Boys' Day, May 5, focuses more on health, lively carp banners fluttering from many a home. In front of the Chinese plate is a Noh dancer, while the figure to the right is of the 16th-century daimyo or feudal lord Takeda Shingen. Below this are brown wooden Japanese kokeshi dolls. Blue and white Chinese ginger jars lift the colour scheme.
Above right: Unpainted wooden door and window frames set a warm, natural tone for Sakata's Asiatic decor. The sturdy wicker armchairs are from the Philippines, but whereas they can often look rather out of place and uncomfortable in a living room, they are here nicely balanced by the cosy comfort of a paisley-covered sofa and Oriental rugs.

Wallace was charmed by the versatility and beauty of bamboo: "When. . . a flat, close floor is required, excellent boards are made by splitting open large bamboos on one side only, and flattening them out so as to form slabs 18 inches [46cm] wide and six feet [1.8m] long. . . . These with constant rubbing of the feet and the smoke of the years become dark and polished, like walnut or old oak, so that their real material can hardly be recognized."

When psycho-anthropologist Lawrence Blair repeated Wallace's epic tour of the Indonesian archipelago over a century later, he had a house built in Bali on traditional lines and so was able to compare it with his Hollywood home. "Successful living in Los Angeles requires controlling the environment, whereas in Bali it requires a total surrender," he wrote in *Ring of Fire*. In Hollywood he lived in a hermetically sealed interior whereas in Bali he had no doors, walls or windows, just reed blinds between him and the surrounding vegetation. In America he was under pressure to buy insecticides; "in Bali it is taboo to move into a new home before the geckos and house-spiders have taken up residence first."

What to the casual onlooker might seem a simplistic primitive construction — "a glorified jungle tree house" — actually demanded careful structural calculation. The native craftsmen, as Blair discovered, knew the critical angle at which an elephant-grass roof would begin to absorb rather than reject rainwater, and the thatch was kept dry through clever exploitation of the cellular structure of the coconut palm which conveys moisture from roots to branches. The eight coconut trunks supporting the house were planted upside down so that they continued "even in death to draw moisture from the roof thatch down into the ground".

Building styles vary throughout Indonesia,

reflecting the mixture of races and religions — Shamanism, Buddhism, Hinduism and Islam — which have fed the cultures of the different islands. Most dramatic are the houses of the Toroja people of Sulawesi. Believing that their ancestors arrived on earth in spaceships, they build their houses in the arc form of the vessels which supposedly deposited them on this planet. In West Java houses are timber framed and stand some 16 inches (40cm) off the ground, the space underneath being used as a chicken run. Floors are of the springy bamboo variety that Wallace so admired, while walls are made of diagonally woven bamboo matting which allows free circulation of air. As elsewhere in Indonesia, nails are never used in construction — instead joints are wedged and wooden pegs hammered into drillholes.

The legacy of animism can still be seen in the heavily decorated Batak houses of Sumatra. Stylized animal heads are carved into the front of the house to ward off evil spirits and the lizard is a widespread feature, either carved into the wood or worked from sugar-palm coir threaded through the walls. Most decorative of all are the Sumatran Minangkabau houses with their multi-gabled roofs and outward-sloping ends, like a ship in full sail. The front and side walls are covered in vertical bands of carved and brightly painted ornamental scrollwork.

The "parasol" construction of buildings, with sloping eaves shading verandahs, is more commonly found in those countries where Buddhism has had most impact, such as Thailand and Korea. It is based on the belief that Buddha found enlightenment while resting under a tree, and that homes are only a temporary shelter while preparing the soul for the afterlife. The house thus emulates the spreading shelter construction of a tree, and uses wood and trunk-pillars in as natural or "unfinished" a state as possible.

Native Indonesian furniture is minimal, the floor being adequate for most activities; the elaborate carved wooden chests from this area are the product of colonial taste — influenced by the Dutch or Portuguese and usually copied by craftsmen from originals in palaces or temples. More authentic are the smaller portable household items used for storage, for example the exquisite closely woven lidded baskets from Lombok, or wonderfully rustic trunks made from banana leaves.

Nowadays fabric has replaced spice as Southeast Asia's exotic hold over the West, with jewel-bright silks from Thailand and superbly animated batiks from Indonesia. Batik is a dye-resist technique, perfected in Java in the 16th century: hot wax is applied to the cloth either with a copper printing-block or, in batik *tulis* ("written" batik), with a tool called a *canting* which is used like a hot-wax pen. For ikat fabrics, in contrast, the yarn is bound into motifs with a colour-resistant fibre and then dyed before it is woven into cloth. Most of the textiles, originally worn as body cloths, are woven on a backstrap loom and therefore quite narrow but the perfect size for a wall-hanging, a touch of Oriental warmth for a modern home.

Right: A magnificent antique Japanese mizuya *chest in cypress wood which would have originally belonged in the formal anteroom where the tea ceremony was prepared; kitchen furniture was much more modest. The antique robe and necklace come from Tibet.*

Java is renowned for its expertise in batik printing; the technique has been in use since the 16th century. Each area has its own distinct patterns, the influence of China on the development of coastal batiks coming across in the designs incorporating birds and flowers, while central Javanese styles tended to become more graphically stylized after conversion to Islam proscribed representation of animals and people. This area of the world offers a wide variety of skilfully crafted baskets — and of course no Asiatic decor is complete without the ubiquitous statue of Buddha.

Peter Adler
191 Sussex Gardens
London W2
England
(By appointment only,
tel 071-262 1775)
Tribal items.

Albrissi
1 Sloane Square
London SW1W 8EE
England
*Modern ethnic and
neoprimitive furniture,
accessories.*

Anta
141 Portland Rd
London W11 4LR
England
*Scottish fabrics,
ceramics.*

Antecs
5812 West Lovers
    Lane
Dallas TX 75225
USA
Cowboy style.

Arcade Gallery
2200 Bodega Ave
Petaluma CA 94952
USA
African arts.

Artesanos
222 Galistea St
Santa Fe NM 87501
USA
*Mexican furniture, folk
art, accessories.*

Artisan
797 Wandsworth Rd
London SW23
England
Rugs, glass, accessories.

**Brisbane
International**
921 Post St
San Francisco
CA 94109
USA
Indonesian art, antiques.

Ceramica Blue
10 Blenheim Crescent
London W11 1NN
England
Mediterranean ceramics.

**Chevignon Trading
Post**
4 rue des Rosiers
75004 Paris
France
*New-Mexican-style
furniture.*

The Conran Shop
Michelin House
81 Fulham Road
London SW3 6RD
England
*Fabrics, furniture,
accessories.*

Davis Gallery
3964 Magazine St
New Orleans
LA 70115
USA
African tribal art.

**The Dining Room
Shop**
62 White Hart Lane
London SW13
England
Furniture.

The Egyptian Touch
76 Goldhawk Rd
London W12
England
*Brass lamps, modern
Egyptian crafts.*

Etamine
63 rue du Bac
75007 Paris
France
Tableware, glass.

Family Shoes
55 Neal St
London WC2
England
Pendleton blankets.

The Folktree
217 South Fairoaks
    Ave
Pasadena
CA 91105
USA
*World folk art,
ceramics, fabrics.*

Frederico
1522 Montana Ave
Santa Monica
CA 90403
USA
*Native American and
Mexican crafts.*

Ganesha
6 Park Walk
Fulham
London SW3
England
Furniture, accessories.

David Gill
60 Fulham Rd
London SW3
England
Neoprimitive furniture.

Global Village
Roundwell St
South Petherton
Somerset
TA13 5AA
England
International crafts.

Joss Graham
10 Eccleston St
London SW1
England
*African and Asian
textiles, tribal art.*

Homestead
222 East Main St
Fredericksburg
TX 98624
USA
Cowboy style.

Paul Hughes
3a Pembridge Square
London W2
England
*African and pre-
Columbian ethnic
textiles.*

Ikea
2 Drury Way
North Circular Road
London NW10
England
Accessories.

Indian Trader West
204 W. San Francisco
Santa Fe NM 87501
USA
Rugs.

Insulinde
PO Box 764
Forest Knolls
CA 94933
USA
*Indonesian antiques,
textiles.*

Kikapu
Africa Centre
38 King St
London WC2
England
*African furniture, rugs,
fabrics, accessories, art.*

Liberty
Regent St
London W1R 6AH
England
and:
Liberty
Rockefeller Center
5th Ave
New York
NY 10020
USA
*Fabrics, furniture, rugs,
accessories.*

**The Life-Enhancing
Tile Company**
Unit 4a
Alliance House
14-28 St Mary's Rd
Portsmouth
Hampshire
England
*Encaustic tiles with
ethnic motifs.*

Ian Mankin
109 Regent's Park Rd
London NW1
and at:
Agnes Bourne
550 15th St
San Francisco
CA 94103
USA
*Simple cotton fabrics in
checks and stripes.*

McKinney Kidston
1 Wandon Rd
London SW6 2JF
England
Swedish ginghams.

Mexique
67 Sheen Lane:
London SW14
England
*Mexican furniture,
accessories.*

**Morning Star
Gallery**
513 Canyon Rd
Santa Fe NM 87501
USA
Native American art.

Muthaiga
1 Park St
Stow-on-the-Wold
Gloucestershire
England
African furniture, textiles.

Neal Street East
5 Neal St
London WC2
England
*Oriental fabrics,
ceramics, cookware,
lamps, basketware.*

Nice Irma's
46 Goodge St
London WIP IFJ
England
*Fabrics, rugs, glass,
accessories.*

Nonesuch Gallery
1211 Montana Gallery
Santa Monica
CA 90405
USA
*Folk, cowboy, Native
American arts, fabrics.*

Old Hickory
403 Noble St
Shelbyville IN 46176
USA
Hickory furniture.

**Omarts, Art
Dealers**
577 2nd St and Brannan
San Francisco
CA 94107
USA
Moroccan furniture.

Rainbow Man
107 E. Palace Ave
Santa Fe
NM 87501
USA
*Old Native American
ceramics, rugs.*

Ravissant
159 Fulham Rd
London SW3
England
Fabrics.

Russian Shop
99 The Strand
London WC2
England
*Russian lacquerware,
shawls.*

**Santa Fe Trading
Post**
34 Bruton Place
London W1
England
*Tableware, bags,
cushions.*

The Shaker Shop
25 Harcourt St
London W1
England
*Fabrics, tableware,
kitchenware.*

Shyam Ahuja
201 East 56th St
Third Ave
New York NY
USA
and at Liberty, England
Indian fabrics.

Le Souk Gallery
1001 East Alameda
Santa Fe
NM 87501
USA
Berber arts.

Souleiado
39 rue Proudhon
BP 21
13151 Tarascon
Cedex
France
and at:
171 Fulham Rd
London SW3 6JW
England
and at:
Pierre Deux
870 Madison Ave
New York
NY 10014
USA
Provençal fabrics.

**Tansu Design
Imports**
Galleria Design Center
101 Henry Adams St
 # 320
San Francisco
CA 94103
USA
*Japanese and Korean
furniture.*

Teixeira Ltd
108 St George's
 Square
London SW1V 3QY
England
Rugs.

True West
Box 48
802 South Austin St
Comanche
TX 76442
USA
*Wholesalers of cowboy
and Native American
print fabrics.*

**The Turkish Craft
Centre**
Unit 2
Blythe Mews
Off Blythe Rd
London W14
England
*Fabrics, copperware,
tiles.*

Ventilo
27 bis, rue du Louvre
75002 Paris
France
*Native American
furniture, accessories.*

Verandah
15b Blenheim Crescent
London
W11 2EE
England
*Fabrics, glass,
tableware, basketware.*

David Wainwright
251 Portobello Rd
London W11
England
*West Rajasthan
antique furniture,
artefacts.*

**Robert Young
Antiques**
68 Battersea Bridge
 Rd
London
SW11 3AG
England
Furniture, folk art.

DESIGNERS

**Christian
Astuguevieille**
10 rue Portalis
Paris 8ème
France
*String-covered furniture
and accessories.*

Thomas Callaway
1000 Gretna Green
 Way
Los Angeles
CA 90049
USA
Furniture.

David Champion
Collett Champion
Fernhead Studios
2b Fernhead Rd
London W9 3ET
England
Interiors.

**Christophe
Decarpentrie**
18 ave des Saisons
Ixelles
Brussels
Belgium
Interiors.

François Gilles
IPL Interiors
308 Fulham Rd
London SW10
England
Furniture.

Nigel Lofthouse
The Old Church
Rishangles
Suffolk IP23 7JZ
England
*African-inspired
furniture, lights.*

Ivy Rosequist
PO Box 410507
San Francisco
CA 94141
USA
*Wicker furniture,
interiors.*

Sandra Sakata
Obiko
794 Sutter
San Francisco CA
USA
Interiors.

Malcolm Temple
36 Trebovir Rd
London SW5
England
Furniture.

Steve Wright
45 Melbourne Grove
East Dulwich
London SE22
England
Decorative design.

INDEX

ARTEFACTS SET DETAILS

COWBOY, pp 44–5: Pendleton blankets from Family Shoes; saddle bag from Santa Fe Trading Post; candlestick from Artisan; spurs from Hyper Hyper; other items courtesy of James Merrell.

NATIVE AMERICAN, pp 54–5: Rug, pots from Morning Star Gallery; all other items courtesy of Chris O'Connell.

MEXICAN, pp 68–9: Rug, tin lunchbox, tin plates, clay pots from Santa Fe Trading Post; sun wall-plaque, tins from Liberty; cross from Artisan.

CELTIC, pp 80–1: All items courtesy of Annie and Lachlan Stewart.

NORDIC, pp 86–7: Checked fabric from McKinney Kidston; basket from Verandah; napkin from Shaker Shop; painted wooden boxes from Ikea; wooden scoops, trays,

table runner, red baskets from Line of Scandinavia.

TYROLEAN, pp 94–5: Gingham from Ian Mankin; chair from Robert Young Antiques; heart-motif chopping board, napkins, lavendar bags, Alpine embroidery from Shaker Shop.

EAST EUROPEAN, pp 100–1: All items from the Russian Shop.

MEDITERRANEAN, pp 108–9: Background fabric, copperware, tiles from The Turkish Craft Centre; jugs, plates from Ceramica Blue; chair from the Dining Room Shop; table fabric from Souleiado.

NORTH AFRICAN, pp 128–9: Moroccan silk/wool rug from Teixeira; ceramics from Verandah; Indian wooden screen from David Wainwright; Egyptian glass from Verandah and Artisan.

TRIBAL, pp 138–9: All items courtesy of Peter Adler.

GOLD COAST, pp 146–7: Appliquéwork fabric from Paul Hughes; all other items from Joss Graham.

JAPANESE, pp 158–9: Checked cloth, iron teapot, Sashiko-stitch fabric from Neal Street East; kimono from Liberty; blue and white porcelain from Neal Street East and Liberty; quilt from The Conran Shop.

INDIAN, pp 166–7: Embroidered cushion, coloured pots from Global Village; saris from Ravissant; silk cushions, red spot-print shawl, wooden spice box, slippers from Liberty; papier mâché bowl from David Wainwright; pots from Verandah; metal plates from Neal Street East.

ASIACTIC, pp 174–5: Indonesian sarongs, tiered basket, birdcage, painted wooden water carriers from Neal Street East; Buddha, lidded basket, rattle, spoons from Global Village; Indonesian shawl from Verandah.

ACKNOWLEDGMENTS

180

It is customary to write particularly sycophantic thankyous to all the people involved in the production of books like this, in the hope that the requisite degree of oiliness will send another book contract sliding the author's way. And who am I to break such an honourable tradition? Judith More, the executive editor, would make an excellent midwife: even when labour had to be induced, the date of delivery a long-distant memory, she retained her imperturbable calm. Thanks also to the surreptitious but effective hand of Cathy Rubinstein in editing the copy, and to the design talents and good humour of Jacqui Small and Trinity Fry. On Katrin Cargill fell the not entirely rewarding task of persuading busy people to open up their doors to the photographer and the even more impossible task of finding, among others, stylish Tyrolean artefacts.

Heartfelt, grease-free thanks to Midori Nishikawa, for letting me loose among her stunning collection of books on Japan; also to Christine Walker for her invaluable help on Indonesia, and to Malcolm Temple, out of whose grip I eventually managed to prise the only book on Thomas Molesworth in the country. The library at the Austrian Institute educated my prejudices about cuckoo clocks. And long live the wonderful National Art Library at the Victoria and Albert Museum — who only failed me on Molesworth.

Now for the really nauseous stuff — the little-woman tributes to supporting husband and neglected children, between the lines of which you are supposed to read what incredibly long hours the author put in. So, thanks Julian for buying all those suppers at Marks & Spencer, and thank you Jonah, Freddie and Maudie for enduring abbreviated bedtime stories and the occasional motherless weekend. Also to number four, whoever you are, for sharing your gestation with this book — if you don't emerge sporting a calabash and wrapped in cross-stitch embroidery it will be a miracle. . . .

The author and publishers would like to thank the following home owners:
Christian Astuguevieille, Teresa and Tyler Beard, Judy and Ennius Bergsma, Thomas Callaway, David Champion, Christophe Decarpentrie, Barbara Dorf, François Gilles, Jacques Grange, Claudia Grau, Linda and Peter Guber, Laura Hunt, Françoise Lafon, Jack Lenor Larsen, Melanie Martin, Issey Miyake, Chris O'Connell, Lars Olsen, Chuck and Jan Rosenak, Ivy Rosequist, Sandra Sakata, Lars Sjoberg, Skansen Museum, Annie and Lachlan Stewart, Malcolm Temple, Zaza Van Hulle, Armand Ventilo, David Wainwright, Steve Weber, Steve Wright.

Left: Part of the appeal of ethnic art lies in its whimsicality. Chuck Rosenak's collection is complemented by a humorous animalistic display, with echoes of childhood boardgames in the ladder handrail leading up to the gallery balustrade entwined with snakes.